LET'S MAKE THE BOOK ABOUT YOU!

Discover your
AI Companion

Meet your AI Companion

Imagine this: you're not just reading this book, but engaging in a direct conversation with it. It feels as though the author is right beside you, ready to answer your questions and support you with his knowledge and expertise. To the left, you'll see how such a conversation with the AI Companion might look. The LannooCampus Companion perfectly adapts the content of *Marketing* to:
- you as a student or professional;
- your company or organisation;
- and your unique situation.

Through a convenient chat feature (available in WhatsApp), you'll discover additional functionalities that go beyond the classic learning experience – such as personalised advice, real-time updates, and practical tools to immediately apply the book's insights.

Experience a new, interactive way of learning that truly grows with you in 3 easy steps:

STEP 1: Go to: https://click.lannoo.be/ai-marketing-eng
or scan the QR code and follow the instructions.

STEP 2: To activate the AI Companion you will need the following unique activation code.

f23eefde424792c1

STEP 3: Open the chat and start the conversation.
You get free access from the moment you register.

T0389756

Marketing

Reinventing the Basics

Igor Nowé

Lannoo Campus

D/2025/45/59 – ISBN 978 90 209 3405 2 – NUR 802

Cover and interior design: LannooCampus
© Cover image: freepik.com
© Igor Nowé & Lannoo Publishers nv, Tielt, 2025.

LannooCampus Publishers is a subsidiary of Lannoo Publishers, the book and multimedia division of Lannoo Publishers nv.

All rights reserved.
No part of this publication may be reproduced and/or made public, by means of printing, photocopying, microfilm or any other means, without the prior written permission of the publisher.

LannooCampus Publishers
Vaartkom 41 box 01.02
3000 Leuven
Belgium

P.O. Box 23202
1100 DS Amsterdam
The Netherlands

www.lannoocampus.com

CONTENTS

Introduction 11

Part 1: Operational marketing

Chapter 1: The basics of "operational marketing": Kotler's 4P 19

Chapter 2: The "evolved" model: SAVE 21

2.1	**Solution** 26	
2.1.1	General 26	
2.1.2	The "needs" model by Maslow 27	
2.1.3	Different layers within the concept solution 34	
2.1.4	Branding 36	
2.1.5	Segmenting – Targeting – Positioning 43	
2.1.6	Overview on "Solution" 54	

2.2	**Access** 54	
2.2.1	General 54	
	2.2.1.1	Access "part 1": information 55
	2.2.1.2	Access "part 2": closing the "deal" 56
	2.2.1.3	Access "part 3": customer service 56
2.2.2	Different types of "Access channels" 57	
2.2.3	Omni-channel 63	
2.2.4	Access channels considerations 67	
2.2.5	Overview on "Access" 68	

2.3	**Education** 69	
2.3.1	General 69	
2.3.2	PESO model 71	
2.3.3	The difference between Communication (Media) and Promotion.. 75	
2.3.4	Content marketing: 3H model of Google 78	
2.3.5	Experience marketing 81	
	2.3.5.1	General 81
	2.3.5.2	Model of Pine and Gilmore 82
	2.3.5.3	Experiences in a "digital" context 88

| 2.3.6 | Overview on "Education" | 88 |

2.4 Value 89
2.4.1 Elements of Value 89
    2.4.1.1 Element 1 of Value: Solution 90
    2.4.1.2 Element 2 of Value: Access 92
    2.4.1.3 Element 3 of Value: Education 94
2.4.2 Price-paradox 97
2.4.3 Overview on "Value" 99

Chapter 3: Customer (Decision) Journey 100

3.1 History and trends 100

3.2 AIDA: the start 101

3.3 The evolution in the CDJ models 103

3.4 Foote, Cone and Belding's matrix/grid 107

3.5 Some important thoughts about the "Customer Decision Journey" 112

3.6 Overview on "Customer Decision Journey" 117

Chapter 4: SAVE & CDJ... the "perfect" marriage 118

4.1 General recommendations 118
4.1.1 First phase: "awareness" through "Solution" & "Education" 119
4.1.2 Second phase: "active evaluation" through "Access" & "Education" 121
4.1.3 Third phase: "closing the deal" through "Access" & "Value" 124
4.1.4 Final phase: "Post purchase evaluation" through "Value", "Access", "Education", & "Solution" 126
4.1.5 Overview 129

4.2 Measuring Value: focus on "trust" factor 129

Chapter 5: Some general remarks 134

5.1   **The era of artificial intelligence** 134

5.2   **B2C vs B2B: same challenges... different settings...** 136
5.2.1   B2B 137
5.2.2   B2C 138

Part 2: Strategic marketing

Chapter 1: General introduction to strategic marketing 143

Chapter 2: Strategic process 145

2.1   **Step 1: Strategic overview** 145
2.1.1   Mission statement.. 146
2.1.2   Vision statement 146
2.1.3   (Strategic) Goals 147
2.1.4   Values.. 148

2.2   **Step 2: External analysis** 149
2.2.1   External analysis: Meso environment...................................... 151
         2.2.1.1   Five Forces Model (Porter).................................... 152
         2.2.1.2   Strategic models (Porter / Treacy & Wiersema)............ 158
         2.2.1.3   Strategy matrices (BCG / GE) 164
         2.2.1.4   General conclusion on Meso environment 170
2.2.2   External analysis: Macro environment 171
         2.2.2.1   DESTEP (or PESTLE)... 171

2.3   **Step 3: Internal analysis** 174
2.3.1   Internal analysis: Micro environment 175
         2.3.1.1   Value Chain model (Porter)...................................175
         2.3.1.2   7S Model (McKinsey) 179
         2.3.1.3   General conclusion on Micro environment 183

2.4   **Step 4: SWOT: the ultimate summary**......................................185

2.5	**Step 5: Going from strategic to operational marketing**	**186**
2.5.1	Strategic options	188
2.5.2	Optimising value	195
	2.5.2.1 (New) Strategic overview	195
	2.5.2.2 (New) Target group: Segmentation – Targeting – Positioning	196
	2.5.2.3 (New) Value proposition – (New) SAVE	196

2.6	**Overview on "strategic planning"**	**197**

Epilogue: The future of Marketing is built on Trust and Value	**199**
Acknowledgements	**203**
Notes	**205**

Introduction:
Marketing... Reinventing the basics

The world of marketing has changed – radically, and at an unprecedented speed. The old frameworks that dominated the marketing landscape for decades simply no longer fit the realities of today's marketplace. We live in an era where digital tools are exploding, customer behaviour is increasingly complex, and B2B companies are more economically important than B2C companies. The traditional models, rooted in the 4Ps or the 6Cs, were designed for a different age. Today, these models no longer reflect the interconnected, fast-paced, and value-driven world in which we operate. In a time where product is far too limiting a concept and where price has taken a back seat to the idea of value, marketing must evolve.

This book, *Marketing... Reinventing the Basics*, invites you to step away from the old ways of thinking and embrace a more contemporary, dynamic approach to marketing. This is not just about tweaking existing models; it's about rethinking the entire foundation of how we approach marketing in today's world. The models and strategies we'll explore in this book are designed to reflect the rapid changes in technology, the shift in how customers make decisions, and the increasing importance of long-term relationships over short-term transactions.

The digital shift and the changing role of B2B

The rise of digital technology has created a world where information is abundant, access is immediate, and customer expectations are higher than ever. The boundaries between products and services are becoming increasingly blurred, as businesses leverage digital tools to deliver unique customer experiences, personalised offers, and interactive engagements. This shift has led to a fundamental change in how we think about the marketing function itself.

In today's business environment, B2B companies – especially those in industries such as technology, healthcare, and professional services – are playing a more significant role than ever before. In fact, B2B companies are economically more important than their B2C counterparts, driving innovation, fuelling economies, and shaping global markets. Yet, even in these traditionally "business-to-business" sectors, the customer experience is now just as critical as in B2C settings. The challenge for marketers today is to redefine their value proposition in ways that resonate with the evolving expectations of business clients who demand personalised, value-driven solutions rather than just generic products.

The limitations of traditional models

For years, marketers have relied on frameworks like the 4Ps (Product, Price, Place, Promotion) and the 6Cs (Customer, Cost, Convenience, Communication, Content, Community) to guide their strategies. These models were groundbreaking in their time, but they were designed for a different era – one of mass production, limited communication channels, and static customer relationships. In today's digital-first world, these models don't fully capture the complexity of customer behaviour or the intricate dynamics of the modern marketplace.

The focus on Value... leading to trust

In this book, we'll explore how to move away from the traditional focus and shift towards creating value. It's no longer simply about offering the lowest price or the most convenient point of purchase; it's about delivering solutions that genuinely meet customer needs, solve their problems, and enhance their lives in ways that feel meaningful. This shift is rooted in a deeper understanding of customer behaviour – today's consumers are not just looking for transactions, but for experiences that make them feel valued, informed, and empowered. As businesses focus on providing value, they cultivate trust – an essential ingredient in the customer journey. Trust, built through consistent value delivery, forms the foundation for deeper customer relationships and becomes the key to driving engagement, loyalty, and advocacy over time.

The digital revolution has created a level of competition and transparency that has forever changed the dynamics between businesses and customers. Digital tools like artificial intelligence, big data, social media, and automation have radically altered the way companies engage with their customers. Marketers now have more access to customer data and insights than before, and with that comes the responsibility to craft marketing strategies that are not just reactive but proactive, anticipatory, and hyper-relevant to customers' ever-changing needs.

Two core parts of the book:
operational and strategic marketing

This book is structured into two key parts, each focusing on a different but equally important aspect of modern marketing: **operational marketing** and **strategic marketing**. The first part of the book delves into the operational side of marketing, where we'll explore two critical models that align with the current digital and customer-driven landscape: the **SAVE Model** and the **Customer Decision Journey**.

The SAVE Model, developed by Harvard Business School, offers a contemporary alternative to traditional marketing frameworks. The model focuses on creating **solutions** for customers, providing them with **access** to your offerings, emphasising the **value** customers derive from your brand, and **educating** them throughout their journey. These four pillars are essential in today's marketplace, where customers are looking for more than just a product – they're looking for comprehensive solutions that add real value to their lives.

In parallel, we will explore the **Customer Decision Journey**, which moves away from the old, linear purchase funnel and embraces the complexity of today's buying process. The decision-making journey is no longer a simple path from awareness to purchase; it's a fluid, dynamic process in which customers continually interact with brands, reassess their needs, and engage in multiple stages before finally making a decision. Understanding this new customer journey is critical for marketers who want to stay ahead of the curve and engage customers at every touchpoint.

The second part of the book focuses on **strategic marketing**, where we explore how to develop comprehensive, long-term marketing plans. Here, we dive into the importance of conducting both external and internal analyses to identify opportunities, threats, and gaps in the marketplace. By understanding the strengths and weaknesses of both your company and the broader market, you can craft strategic plans that align with customer needs and organisational goals.

Through the lens of **SWOT analysis**, you'll learn how to identify where your organisation stands in relation to the competition and how to pivot or adapt your strategies accordingly. While the operational elements of marketing focus on the tactical and immediate, strategic marketing ensures that those actions align with

Introduction

long-term objectives, building sustainable growth and value for both the company and its customers.

Why reinventing marketing matters now more than ever

The rapid pace of change in the marketing world means that what worked in the past simply doesn't work today. Digital tools, shifting customer expectations, and the increasing prominence of B2B companies have made the old marketing models obsolete. The market is no longer defined by static products, set prices, and fixed customer segments. Instead, it's driven by a dynamic interplay of value creation, personalised experiences, and long-term relationships.

As you read through the chapters ahead, this book will challenge you to rethink the very foundation of marketing – to shift from old paradigms to new, more flexible, and more relevant ways of engaging with customers. By reinventing the basics, you'll be better equipped to navigate the complexities of today's marketing landscape and create strategies that deliver real value to your customers and your business.

I wish you a very pleasant journey into the inspiring world called "marketing".

Part 1: Operational marketing

Chapter 1:
The basics of "operational marketing": Kotler's 4P

As described above, marketing as a "science" really started to develop from the second half of the last century once people switched to a consumer society, leading to the development of brands. A useful tool here was **Philip Kotler's 4P model**, also called the "**marketing mix**".[1]

This model was introduced in the 1960s. This timeless framework has become a cornerstone in the field of marketing, providing a comprehensive guide for businesses to formulate and implement successful marketing strategies.

The 4Ps represent the key elements of a marketing strategy, each playing a crucial role in achieving a company's objectives:
a. **Product:** At the core of the 4P model is the product itself. Kotler emphasised the importance of understanding and developing a product that meets the needs and desires of the target market. This involves not only the physical attributes of the product but also its design, packaging, branding, and overall value proposition. A well-conceived product is the foundation upon which successful marketing strategies are built.
b. **Price:** The pricing element of the model focuses on determining the right price for the product or service. Kotler emphasised the need to strike a balance between setting a price that reflects the product's value and aligning with the financial expectations of the target market. Pricing strategies may involve cost-based, value-based or competitive pricing and the chosen approach directly influences consumer perceptions and market positioning.
c. **Place:** The "Place" component of the 4Ps addresses the distribution channels and methods by which the product reaches the consumer. Kotler stressed the importance of selecting the most effective channels to ensure the product is readily available to the target audience. This involves considerations such as the choice of retail outlets, online platforms, logistics and supply chain management. A strategic placement enhances accessibility and contributes to overall customer satisfaction.
d. **Promotion:** Promotion encompasses all the activities a company undertakes to communicate and promote its product to the target market. This in-

cludes advertising, public relations, sales promotions, and personal selling. Kotler highlighted the significance of creating a compelling and consistent message that resonates with the target audience. Successful promotion builds brand awareness, generates interest and ultimately drives sales.

The Kotler's 4P model offers a structured and versatile approach to marketing, aiding businesses in developing effective strategies that are customer-focused, adaptable and aligned with organisational objectives. It is simple, structured and easy to use... and millions of marketers have used it (or perhaps are still using it) to frame their marketing activities and plans.

But from the 1990s, the world experienced an accelerated degree of digitalisation that completely changed commercial needs and everything linked to them, such as communication and consumer behaviour. Kotler's 4P model wasn't adapted to this revolution in marketing:
a. The model may not fully address the complexities of digital marketing and online platforms prevalent in today's landscape.
b. The model was primarily designed for tangible products, making it less adaptable to service-oriented businesses.
c. The model is transaction-focused and may not sufficiently address the modern marketing emphasis on building strong, lasting customer relationships.
d. The model oversimplifies marketing decisions, potentially overlooking the interconnected nature of modern marketing and with a higher emphasis on the "pricing" element.
e. In fast-paced markets, the model may lack the agility needed to adapt quickly to changing consumer behaviours.

It's clear that the 4P model as such needs some updating to be useful for the modern marketer.

Chapter 2:
The "evolved" model: SAVE

Figure 1.1: 4Ps are changed into SAVE [2]

In 2013 some marketing experts (Ettenson, Conrado and Knowles) published an article in the Harvard Business Review, titled "Rethinking the 4Ps", in which they describe a more "modern" version of Kotler's traditional 4P model.[3] They described their marketing framework as "**SAVE**":

a. SOLUTION

b. ACCESS

c. VALUE

d. EDUCATION

Essentially, it comes down to the fact that the classic 4Ps are no longer adequate in this digital world and can be better defined as SAVE:

"**Product**" becomes "**Solution**". As a marketer, you'd better define the offerings by needs, not by features, function or technological superiority.

"**Place**" becomes "**Access**". As marketer you need to develop an integrated omni-channel presence that considers customers' entire purchase journey instead of emphasising individual purchase locations and channels.

"**Price**" becomes "**Value**". Rather than stressing how price relates to production costs, profit margins or competitors' prices, it would be better to articulate the benefits relative to price.

"**Promotion**" becomes "**Education**". As a marketer you'd better Provide information relevant to customers' specific needs at each point of the purchase cycle or customer journey, rather than relying on advertising, PR, and personal selling.

It's clear that this SAVE model tackles certain of the above-mentioned disadvantages of the traditional 4Ps model. SAVE is more in line with the digital world around us, more focused on customer-centricity and on service-related marketing. In the next chapters, we're going to describe each element of the model more in detail.

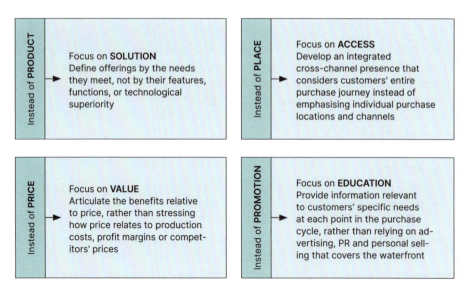

Figure 1.2: SAVE model [4]

Some extra information: Kahneman's Principles[5]

Let's start with a small riddle...

"A tennis racket and a ball cost €5.10 in total. The racket costs €5.00 more than the ball. How much does the ball cost?"

If you think the answer is €0.10, you'd better read this paragraph to understand why you think this might be the answer.

To get some insights into "consumer behaviour", which is important in marketing, you need to understand how our human brain functions. In his groundbreaking book, *Thinking, Fast and Slow*, Nobel prize laureate Daniel Kahneman introduces the concept of two distinct systems that govern human thought processes: System 1 and System 2. These systems represent different modes of thinking, each with its own characteristics, strengths, and potential pitfalls.

System 1: Fast Thinking

It's the intuitive, automatic, and rapid-thinking system. It operates effortlessly, requiring little conscious effort or control. This system is responsible for quick, snap judgements and reactions in everyday situations. It relies on heuristics, mental shortcuts that enable swift decision-making based on past experiences and patterns.

System 1 is invaluable for routine tasks and scenarios where immediate responses are necessary, saving cognitive resources.

System 2: Slow Thinking

In contrast, System 2 is the deliberate, conscious, and slow-thinking system. It engages in more effortful cognitive processes, requiring focus and mental energy.

System 2 comes into play when faced with complex problems, unfamiliar situations, or when a more thoughtful and analytical approach is needed. It involves careful consideration, logical reasoning, and the weighing of evidence.

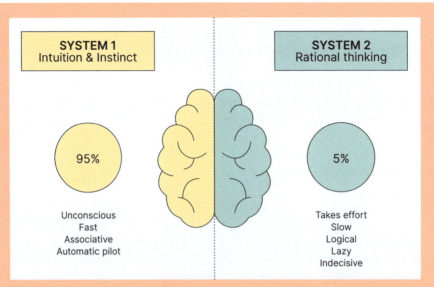

Figure 1.3: System 1 and System 2 thinking by Kahneman [6]

While System 2 allows for more accurate and rational decision-making, it has limitations. It can be resource-intensive, and people often default to the more automatic System 1 thinking to conserve mental energy. Additionally, System 2 is not immune to errors, and its capacity for sustained attention is finite.

One striking observation from Kahneman's research is that although System 2 is far more reliable than System 1, System 2 is inherently lazy. That is to say, if the information to make a decision appears to be available at System 1, System 2 will happily leave that responsibility to System 1 and remain idle.

Let's get back to our introductory riddle to explain the difference between System 1 and 2:

"A tennis racket and a ball cost €5.10 in total. The racket costs €5.00 more than the ball. How much does the ball cost?"

If you said that the ball cost 10 cents, you aren't alone. But you'd be incorrect. If the ball costs 10 cents, then the racket would cost €5.10 ("The racket

costs €5.00 more than the ball."), which would total €5.20 breaking the stated constraints *("A tennis racket and a ball cost €5.10 in total.")*.
The answer is that the ball costs 5 cents (consequently, the racket costs €5.05).

Part of the reason for this laziness is the sheer availability of information from System 1. The speed with which we are able to respond to changing circumstances with this voluntary system is far greater than the effort required to engage and leverage the logic of System 2.

Another reason for this laziness is the physical energy required to support System 2. The brain uses more energy when we are conducting tasks that rely heavily on System 2. As we lean on System 2 more, we may feel some kind of "decision fatigue" and are more likely to fall back on readily available information at System 1.

These principles are crucial in our quest for how to take potential consumers on a journey to convince them to buy certain products, knowing full well that 95% of their decisions are made according to System 1 and only 5% through the more "data-driven" and "energy-consuming" System 2.

Or put another way... in the majority of decisions, consumers are guided by their "emotions" ("it looks good") more than by their own "rationale" based on data.

Knowing this, the use of SAVE as a marketing model leans closer to the fact that consumers use System 1 ("faster" and "more intuitive" way of thinking) more often, whereas the 4Ps model focuses too much on the System 2 ("rational") way of decision-making.

Chapter 2: The "evolved" model: SAVE

2.1 Solution

2.1.1 General

The "**Solution**" aspect emphasises a shift from merely selling products to providing solutions to customers' problems. It involves understanding the customer's needs and challenges and offering a comprehensive solution that goes beyond the features of a product. The goal is to create value by addressing specific pain points and delivering outcomes that align with the customer's goals.

The focus on "Solution" might involve considerations related to product development, innovations and how businesses can differentiate themselves by offering solutions that truly meet the needs of their target audience. This way of thinking could include discussions on:
a. **Problem solving:** how well the product, service or brand addresses a particular problem or challenge faced by customers.
b. **Innovations:** creating solutions that stand out in the market and provide a competitive advantage.
c. **Customisation:** tailoring solutions to meet the specific requirements of different customer segments or individual customers.
d. **Added value elements:** going beyond the core product features to provide additional value through services, support or complementary offerings.
e. **Customer-centric approach:** placing the customer at the centre of the solution development process, ensuring that the final product or service truly meets their expectations and needs.

The concept of a "solution" transcends the boundaries of products or services; it extends to encompass a holistic approach that incorporates brands, experiences, people,... and a profound understanding of **customer needs**. In a rapidly evolving business landscape, companies are realising that the true essence of providing a solution lies in crafting a comprehensive and seamless journey for their customers. It involves anticipating and addressing not just the immediate needs but also the latent desires and aspirations of consumers.

Figure 1.4: Needs and solutions

Understanding this complex matter of consumer behaviour will be further explained in the next section: Maslow's hierarchy of needs.

2.1.2 The "needs" model by Maslow

In 1943, Abraham Maslow proposed one of the most cognitively contagious ideas in the behavioural sciences, namely the "hierarchy of human needs".[7] It is a motivational theory in psychology comprising a five-tier model of human needs. The five levels are as follows:

a. **Physiological needs**: these are the basic necessities for survival, such as air, water, food, shelter and sleep. Until these needs are satisfied, an individual's focus is primarily on meeting these essential requirements.

b. **Safety and security**: this includes physical safety (protection from harm), financial stability, health and wellness and a sense of stability and order in their environment.

c. **Love and belonging**: once the lower-level needs are met, people crave social interaction, relationships and a sense of belonging. This includes family, friendship, intimacy and a sense of connection with others.

d. **Self-esteem**: this level involves the desire for self-esteem and the esteem of others. It includes the need for achievement, recognition, status and a positive self-image. People strive for a sense of competence and mastery in their activities.

e. **Self-actualisation**: at the top of the pyramid is the concept of self-actualisation, representing the realisation of one's full potential and personal growth.

This involves pursuing and fulfilling one's unique capabilities, creativity and talents. It is a continual process of becoming the most that one can be.

Although Maslow never visualised his theory in a pyramid, this picture makes it very easy to project the different need layers:

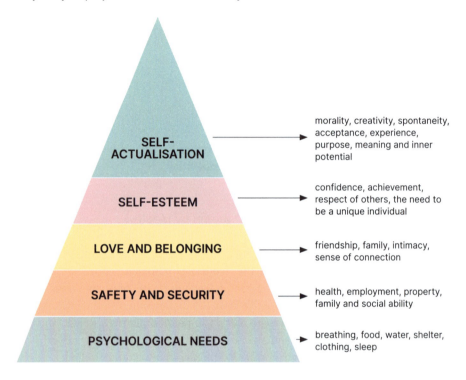

Figure 1.5: Model of human needs (by Maslow) [8]

According to Maslow, the hierarchy suggests that individuals are motivated to fulfil basic needs before moving on to higher-level needs. The order of the levels is not completely fixed. For some, esteem outweighs love, while others may self-actualise despite poverty. Our behaviours are usually motivated by multiple needs simultaneously.

Referring back to the SAVE model and more particularly to the "Solution" part, it's clear that this part corresponds closely to this hierarchical model of needs. Certain solutions are more focused on "physiological" needs where others tap into love and belonging and still others might help consumers to fulfil the need of "self-actualisation". Moreover, it's obvious that "solutions" that aim for "higher" levels of needs are considered more "valuable", which will be tackled in a later section.

> ### Example: The evolution in communication tools and the growing affect on needs and value
>
> Smartphones have transformed communication and consumer needs, extending beyond basic social connections.
>
> Initially, traditional communication tools like telephones fulfilled the **need for love** and belonging, helping people stay in touch. However, smartphones now address higher levels of Maslow's hierarchy. They serve **esteem needs** through status symbols like iPhones and social media validation. They also support **self-actualisation** by offering tools for personal growth, learning, creativity, and productivity. With apps for everything from fitness to education, smartphones help individuals achieve their fullest potential, making them key to both social and personal development in the modern world. This evolution in need satisfaction increased the "value" for this type of "solution".
>
> The same parallel can be drawn with the rise of automobiles over the past centuries.

In the 1960s and early 1970s, most solutions were simply "products" that focused on the physiological (or basic) needs of consumers, which reaffirms the existence of "Product" in Kotler's 4P model.

During the late '70s and '80s, you see "brands" playing a growing role in the evolution of marketing. The more prosperous and developed society becomes, the higher the interest of business in the pursuit of solutions, which leads to higher levels of needs. In the graph on the following page, you can distinguish this "rise of brands", continuing until today and a clear shift from "Classic Companies" (offering "products") to "Platform Companies" (offering "services" and "social values").

Chapter 2: The "evolved" model: SAVE

Figure 1.6: The ten most valuable companies from 1995 to 2018 by market capitalisation in billion US dollars (fortiss GmbH, 2016; Kempe, 2011; Payment & Banking, 2019)[9]

It's clear that this economic evolution goes hand in hand with the growth of "brands" and the rising evolution of advertising spend. "Brands" are simplified "shortcuts of attributes, benefits, beliefs and values that differentiate, reduce complexity and simplify decision-making". Consumers are putting more value on "brands", as it gives them a certain "trust" and it helps them to fulfil (higher) needs.

> **Some extra information: Brands according to Kahneman's theory**
>
> According to Daniel Kahneman's theory of dual-system thinking, consumers make decisions using two systems: **System 1** (fast, intuitive, and automatic) and **System 2** (slow, deliberate, and rational).
>
> Brands play a critical role in influencing System 1 thinking because they provide quick, emotionally driven cues that simplify decision-making. When consumers encounter a brand, they often rely on past experiences, percep-

tions, or emotional associations – like trust, status, or comfort – rather than engaging in detailed analysis.

This reliance on System 1 makes brands important, as they serve as shortcuts for decision-making, reducing cognitive load and making choices feel safer and more familiar.

Example: The world of fashion and "teenagers"

Figure 1.7: A range of fashion trainers of various brands on display [10/11]

During adolescence, the need for acceptance and belonging drives many of the fashion choices teenagers make. Between the ages of 12 and 18, teens are highly influenced by their peer groups – and fashion becomes a way to signal membership in those groups. Wearing certain brands like Nike or Adidas isn't just about the quality of the product but about fitting into a social circle and gaining validation from peers. For example, Adidas, with its iconic sneakers like Stan Smiths or Samba, is not just about comfort or performance. It's a brand that signals membership in sports, streetwear, or even sneaker culture – appealing to teens who want to align with a particular lifestyle. Collaborations with high-profile celebrities like Lionel Messi make Adidas even more aspirational, driving its popularity among teens eager to gain social status.

The need to belong means that the "cool" brands can change quickly. One year, Abercrombie & Fitch or Superdry might dominate, and the next, brands like Carhartt or Dr. Martens take over. These shifts are driven by a desire to keep up with peers and remain socially accepted. Ultimately, for teenagers, fashion brands serve as a way to express identity, stay relevant and feel connected to others.

As mentioned above, the higher the need you fulfil as a brand, the more value a consumer attributes to that brand. Some examples to prove this theory:

- **"Premiumisation"** is a trend that confirms the success of this way of marketing. It's clear that luxury cars like Ferrari or Porsche are tapping into needs like "self-esteem", by offering solutions that make the buyer "stand out" from the crowd (being a unique individual). The fact that they are faster than normal cars is not the main objective of these car brands.
- The current **"sustainability"** trend of so many "solutions" is proven by Maslow's hierarchy model. By choosing more sustainable options, consumers are contributing to a better world in the long-term (safety and security need). As sustainable brands have a higher value to consumers, certain marketers of brands focusing on "primary needs" (physiological needs) like "food or drinks" are adding this element into their brand image.
- **"Customisation"** lets consumers create products that reflect their personal style and preferences, tapping into their need for self-esteem and **self-actualisation**. By personalising items – whether it's a car, clothing, or tech – consumers feel a sense of pride and ownership, boosting their self-worth. This process also allows them to express their individuality and create something that aligns with their identity or aspirations, helping fulfil the need for self-actualisation. Customisation, therefore, strengthens the emotional connection to the brand (= higher "value") and fosters deeper loyalty.

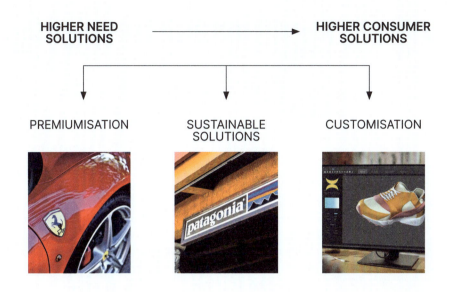

Figure 1.8: Tapping into higher "consumer needs" creates more "consumer value" [12/13/14]

Certain **innovations** have clearly helped consumers to reach their need for "self actualisation", at least partially. For example, mobile phone technology made it possible to be connected with everyone, regardless of time and space. Or even a step further, thanks to social media and smartphones. As a person, you could be part of this vast network of connectivity, giving lots of opportunities (both private and professional). Brands embracing this technological revolution – like Nokia, Meta or Apple – are valued by the international community. By the way, "value" is not only price-related. A lot of Google solutions are free though the brand has a "priceless" value to us all. More about it in the coming section, "Value".

Example: ChatGPT... the innovation that made people "creative"...

Figure 1.9: ChatGPT (OpenAI) [15]

With the launch of ChatGPT by OpenAI in November 2022, everyone now has a powerful tool to enhance their creativity, unlocking new possibilities for self-expression and personal growth. By offering instant access to ideas, feedback, and inspiration, ChatGPT enables individuals to tap into their potential, helping them achieve their goals and fulfil their self-actualisation needs. Whether it's writing, problem-solving, or exploring new interests, this AI-driven platform empowers users to push boundaries and realise their fullest creative potential.

2.1.3 Different layers within the concept solution

In previous sections, we explained the role of "solution" for marketing: marketers are trying to solve certain pains or desires that exist amongst customers based on their needs. In general, you can differentiate 3 types of solutions:
    a. Tangible or physical solutions (e.g. product, ...)
    b. Intangible solutions (e.g. service, ...)
    c. A mix of both a) and b) (e.g. brands, ...).

The type of solution is closely related to the need state, according to Maslow's hierarchy model. It's clear that "physiological needs" or even "safety and security" will be fulfilled by tangible solutions, whereas for more complex needs like "love or belonging" or "self-esteem" customers will go for intangible solutions (brands or services).

In general, Kotler distinguishes **5 different layers around the concept of "product"** and similarly to the concept of "solution", based on customer needs, customer wants and customer demands:[16]

1. **Core benefit:** The core benefit is the basic need or want that the customer satisfies when they buy the solution. For example, "mobility" is a need of someone who wants to go from A to B.
2. **Generic solution:** The generic solution is a basic version made up of only those features necessary for it to function. In the example above, you can think about a car as a possible solution for that person.
3. **Expected solution:** The expected solution includes additional features that the customer might expect. In the mobility example, the customer expects that this car will be safe and secure.
4. **Augmented solution:** The augmented solution refers to any product variations or extra features that might help differentiate the product from its competitors and make the brand a clearer choice amongst the competition. Here you can add some intangible features around the car: a specific car brand (so that the person can express a certain image), all types of services related to the use of that car, special features on that car.
5. **Potential solution:** The potential solution includes all augmentations and improvements the solution might experience in the future. This means that to continue to surprise and delight customers the product must be constantly improved. In the example, this could mean becoming more sustainable, self-driving cars or other technological developments.

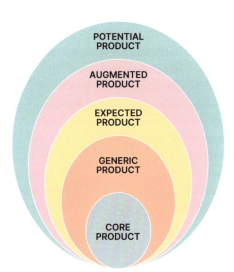

Kotler's Five Product Levels Model

POTENTIAL PRODUCT: Provides additional tangible and intangible features. This refers to the augmentations and transformations that the product may undergo in the future.
AUGMENTED PRODUCT: Product gives more than physical product. This refers to all the additional factors which set the product apart from competition, that is its brand identity and image.
EXPECTED PRODUCT: Offers generic product plus other attributes consumers want. This refers to all the benefits consumers expect to get when they purchase a product.
GENERIC PRODUCT: Provides actual product with tangible qualtities. This represents all the qualities of the product.
CORE PRODUCT: Fulfils basic benefit consumers want. This refers to the basic product. Here, the focus is on the purpose for which the product is intended.

Figure 1.10: Product levels model by Kotler [17]

It's clear that the higher the layer you're aiming for with your solution, the more needs you will possibly fulfil for your customer and the more value you will give to them. This is exactly what a perfect "branding" strategy wants to achieve: it doesn't stick to the tangible features like packaging, but adds intangible layers to it like quality, image, style, … to add more value to it. This will be further explained within the section "Value".

2.1.4 Branding

One way to offer your solution to your customer/consumer is to build it up as a "**brand**". Brands help businesses to build trust in their consumers and to stand out in the market. A strong brand communicates uniqueness, whether through product features, values, or customer experience, which will create a way to "differentiate" your solution from competitors.

Brands evoke emotions. People connect with brands that align with their needs, values, aspirations, or lifestyle. These emotional bonds lead to loyalty and advocacy.

Considering all these advantages of branding, it's clear that brands create more "value" for business and consumers, as increasingly they tap into the higher layers in the Maslow needs model. In the end, people buy brands, not just products.

There are some interesting models around "branding", which will be explained in the following paragraphs:
- CBBE Model (Keller)
- Diamond Model (Kapferer)

a. CBBE model

Kevin Lane Keller developed the **Customer-Based Brand Equity (CBBE) model**.[18] This model is a framework that helps marketers understand and build strong brands by focusing on the customer's perspective. The CBBE model is often represented as a pyramid with four levels and six building blocks.

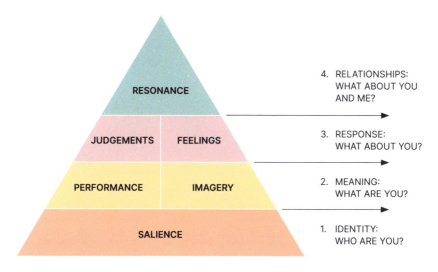

Figure 1.11: CBBE model by Keller

1. **Brand Identity (Who are you?)**
   Salience: This is the foundational level of the pyramid. It refers to the awareness of the brand, ensuring that customers can recognise and recall the brand under different conditions. The goal is to create broad and deep brand awareness.
2. **Brand Meaning (What are you?)**
   Performance: This block focuses on the product's actual performance in terms of quality, reliability, durability, serviceability, and style. It's about meeting consumers' functional needs.
   Imagery: This involves the intangible aspects of the brand, such as the way it meets customers' psychological and social needs. It includes brand personality, values, history, and user profiles.
3. **Brand Response (What about you?)**
   Judgements: This block involves consumers' personal opinions and evaluations of the brand. It includes brand quality, credibility, consideration, and superiority.
   Feelings: This relates to the emotional responses and reactions consumers have towards the brand. It includes feelings like warmth, fun, excitement, security, social approval, and self-respect.
4. **Brand Relationships (What about you and me?)**
   Resonance: At the top of the pyramid, brand resonance represents the ultimate relationship and level of identification the consumer has with the brand.

It includes behavioural loyalty (repeat purchases), attitudinal attachment (love for the brand), sense of community (feeling of belonging), and active engagement (willingness to invest time, money, or other resources in the brand).

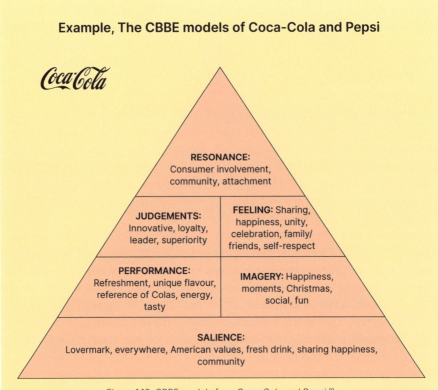

Figure 1.12: CBBE models from Coca-Cola and Pepsi [19]

When comparing Coca-Cola and Pepsi using the CBBE model, we see distinct differences across each of the brand equity elements.

In terms of Brand Salience, Coca-Cola is a lovebrand icon, widely recognised for its long (American cultural) history, while Pepsi, though highly visible, is often seen as Coca-Cola's challenger with a slightly younger, more contemporary and fun feel. In terms of Brand Performance, Coca-Cola is associated with its classic, consistent taste and timeless refreshment, while Pepsi is marketed as sweeter, bolder, and more aligned with those seeking a lively, modern flavour.

Looking at Brand Imagery, Coca-Cola evokes feelings of nostalgia, happiness, and tradition, often linked to family moments and celebrations, such as its iconic holiday advertisements.

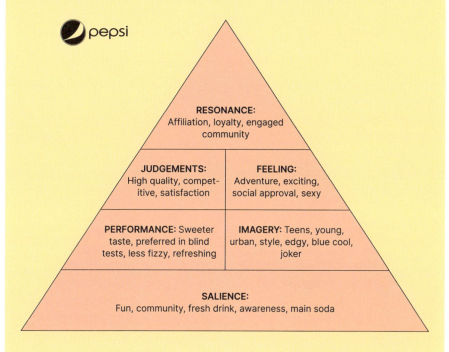

Pepsi, on the other hand, has cultivated an image of youth, energy, and rebellion, frequently associating itself with music, pop culture, and trendsetters through celebrity endorsements like Beyoncé and Michael Jackson.

In terms of Brand Judgements, Coca-Cola is seen as the trusted, original cola brand, known for its consistency and long-standing quality. Pepsi is viewed as more dynamic, attracting consumers who appreciate boldness and a modern appeal. Finally, in Brand Resonance, Coca-Cola enjoys deep emotional connections, often tied to personal memories and significant life

Chapter 2: The "evolved" model: SAVE

moments, leading to high brand loyalty. Pepsi resonates with a younger, trend-driven audience, tapping into lifestyle choices and the desire to be part of a cool, contemporary social group.

Overall, Coca-Cola is positioned as the classic, dependable brand, symbolising tradition and happiness, while Pepsi is the vibrant, youthful alternative, focused on excitement, pop culture, and modernity.

The model elaborated by Keller proposed the following steps, which will lead to "trust":
- Ensure the brand stands out and is easily recognisable
- Develop a strong, positive brand image by meeting customers' functional and psychological needs
- Build positive customer judgements and emotional responses.
- Foster deep, emotional connections and loyalty with customers.

b. Diamond model
The Brand Identity Prism, also known as the Diamond model, is another framework for understanding and building brand identity. Developed by Jean-Noël Kapferer, this model consists of six elements that form a prism, representing the multifaceted nature of brand identity. These elements are divided into two dimensions:
- external (what the brand projects to the outside world)
- internal (what the brand internally represents).

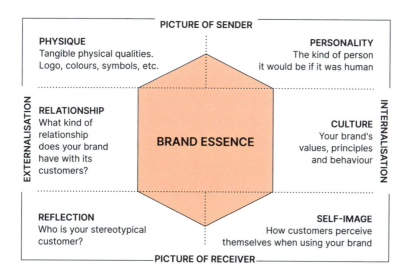

Figure 1.13: Brand Identity Prism / Diamond Model by Kapferer [21]

1. **Physique:** This is the **tangible and physical aspect** of the brand, including the brand's logo, packaging, product features, and design.
   Objective: To create a clear and distinct visual identity that consumers can recognise and associate with the brand.
2. **Personality:** This refers to the brand's character and the **human traits** it embodies. It's about defining the brand as if it were a person, including its tone, style, and behaviour.
   Objective: To develop a unique brand persona that resonates with the target audience.
3. **Culture:** This represents the **values, beliefs, and principles** that underpin the brand. It includes the brand's heritage, country of origin, and core values.
   Objective: To instil a set of values that guide the brand's actions and help differentiate it from competitors.
4. **Relationship:** This element describes the relationship between the brand and its consumers. It includes the **nature of the interactions and the type of bond** the brand seeks to build with its audience.
   Objective: To create meaningful and lasting connections with consumers.

5. **Reflection:** This is the **perceived image** of the brand's typical user. It's about how the brand portrays its target audience in its communications.
   Objective: To ensure that the brand reflects the aspirations and self-image of its customers.
6. **Self-Image:** This represents the **internal mirror of the consumer's own self-perception** when using the brand. It's about how consumers see themselves as a result of using the brand.
   Objective: To enhance customers' self-concept through brand association.

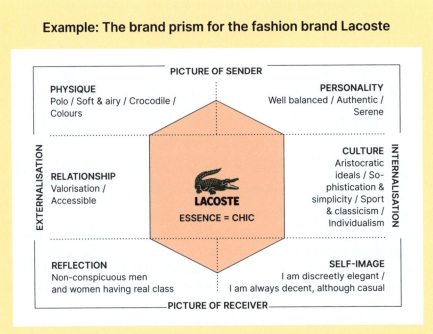

Figure 1.14: Brand prism of Lacoste [22]

Lacoste's brand identity is shaped by its iconic physique, with the signature polo shirts and crocodile logo symbolising casual elegance. The brand's personality is sporty, authentic, and timeless, blending luxury with a relaxed, serene style.

Lacoste's culture is rooted in French heritage and tennis (aristocratic ideals), representing a legacy of merging sport with classicism. The relationship with consumers is built on offering both comfort and style, connecting with those who value sophistication in everyday life.

Lacoste's reflection resonates with individuals who embrace a high-quality, aspirational lifestyle that is both active and classy.

Finally, Lacoste's self-image reflects confidence and style, appealing to those who see themselves as elegant and casual.

2.1.5 Segmenting – Targeting – Positioning

In the previous sections, we've described the link between solutions, the needs related to these and how this can be used in "branding". The next step is now to focus on the possible groups of consumers for whom these needs might be relevant to obtain **target groups**. Understanding needs and its target groups is crucial for marketers in order to obtain the desired consumer behaviour. This exercise is known as the STP model, standing for "Segmentation – Targeting – Positioning".

S	T	P
SEGMENTATION	**TARGETING**	**POSITIONING**
Divide market into distinct groups of customers (segments) using segmentation practices.	Determine which customer group (segment) to focus your marketing efforts on.	Create product positioning and marketing mix that is most likely to appeal to the selected audience.

Figure 1.15: STP model [23]

Chapter 2: The "evolved" model: SAVE

a. **Segmentation**

Segmentation involves dividing a broad market into smaller, more homogeneous groups of consumers who have similar needs, behaviours, or characteristics. The purpose of segmentation is to identify distinct groups within a market that can be targeted with specific marketing strategies.

The segmentation itself starts by choosing the variables to segment the market. The most common groups of segmentation variables are:
a. geographic
b. demographic
c. psychographic
d. behavioural

More details on which elements can be found under each segmentation variable are shown in Figure 1.16 on the following page.

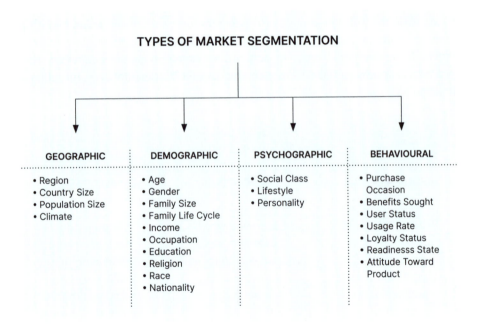

Figure 1.16: Segmentation variables [24]

Once you have chosen the variables that might be interesting for your type of solution, you can form **segments**. You try to group your total market consumers into segments based on the identified criteria, ensuring each segment is **distinct** (one consumer can only be in one segment and not in several) and **significant** (considerable enough and possible to reach).

In general, you will split up your total customer base into different "segments" based on certain "measurable" criteria.

Ideally, after doing this activity, you try to make up "**personas**" for each segment. These are detailed and fictional representations of idealised customers within a segment. These personas encapsulate demographic information, behaviours, preferences, and pain points.

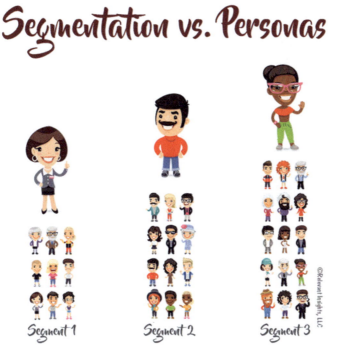

Figure 1.17: Segmentation vs personas [25]

Example: Segment and persona

- **Segment**: A fitness apparel company identifies a segment of health-conscious young adults aged 20-35 who live in urban areas and regularly participate in fitness activities.

- **Persona**: Within this segment, they create a persona named "Urban health freak"... a 26-year-old marketing professional who attends yoga classes three times a week, follows fitness influencers on social media, values eco-friendly products, and prefers shopping online for their workout gear. They have a busy life (both private and professional), though they don't want to feel "stressed".

By personifying key segments, companies can empathise with their customers, tailor products and services to meet specific needs, and refine marketing strategies (which is called "targeting"), ultimately enhancing customer satisfaction and driving overall business success.

Some extra information: Segmenting through the RFM variables

Companies with lots of data about their customer very often use the RFM segmentation. RFM (Recency, Frequency, Monetary) analysis is a customer segmentation technique used to evaluate and categorise customers based on their purchasing behaviour. It helps businesses understand and segment their customer base by identifying patterns in how recently customers have purchased, how often they purchase, and how much they spend. Here's the reasoning behind this analysis.

a. **Recency (R)**:
   - It measures how recently a customer made a purchase.
   - Recent customers are more likely to respond to new promotions

and remain engaged with the brand.

b. **Frequency (F)**:
- It measures how often a customer makes a purchase within a specific period.
- Frequent customers are generally more loyal and can provide consistent revenue.

c. **Monetary (M)**:
- It measures how much money a customer spends on purchases.
- High-spending customers contribute significantly to the company's revenue.

You can start your segmentation exercise by giving each customer a score between 1 and 5 on the variables R, F and M. Combine the RFM scores to create customer segments.

Example: a customer with an RFM score of 555 would be a highly valuable customer (recent, frequent, and high spending), while a customer with a score of 111 would be a low-value customer. A customer with a score of 151 is a customer who buys very regularly, but hasn't bought anything recently and with limited value.

b. Targeting

Targeting involves evaluating the attractiveness of each market segment and selecting one or more segments to focus marketing efforts on. This step is about determining which segments are the most viable and profitable to pursue.

First you need to evaluate attractiveness of each segment. Assess them based on criteria such as segment size, growth potential, profitability, and compatibility with the company's objectives and resources.

Then you will need to select the target segments. Choose only those that present the best opportunities for the company.

Figure 1.18: Marketing targeting strategies [26]

There are four main targeting strategies that companies can use to reach different segments of the market: **undifferentiated**, **differentiated**, **concentrated**, and **micromarketing**.

1. **Undifferentiated Strategy**: This approach targets the entire market with a single marketing effort, assuming that all consumers have similar needs. It's typically used for basic, widely used products, like salt or sugar, where one standard offering can appeal to the majority of consumers.
2. **Differentiated Strategy**: In this strategy, companies target multiple segments and tailor their offerings for each group. The goal is to meet the distinct needs of different consumer segments, increasing the relevance of the product. For example, **Nike** markets its products differently to athletes, fitness enthusiasts, and casual sneaker buyers. Each group is targeted with unique messaging and product features, such as performance-oriented shoes for athletes and stylish, comfortable sneakers for everyday wear.
3. **Concentrated Strategy**: A concentrated strategy focuses on one specific market segment. Companies using this approach often have limited resources and aim to dominate a niche market. **Nike** could use a concentrated strategy to focus specifically on high-performance running shoes for marathon runners. By dedicating resources to this specific group, Nike can develop specialised products and build strong brand loyalty within this niche.
4. **Micromarketing**: This is the most targeted strategy, where companies focus on very small segments or even individual consumers. Using detailed data, brands can personalise their marketing efforts, offering highly tailored messages or customised products. **Nike** employs micromarketing through its **NikeID** service, where customers can personalise their shoes, choosing

colours and features. Nike also uses personalised recommendations and targeted ads based on individual browsing and purchase histories.

The more (digital) data a brand possesses the better they can target consumers with personalised content, on an individual level, aka micromarketing.

c. Positioning

After having segmented your consumer group and taking any targeting decisions, you need to **position** your solution on the market. It's all about creating a distinct and valued solution in the minds of the target consumers. It involves defining how the solution is different from competitors and how it fulfils the needs of the target segment(s).

The best way to proceed is to make up a **positioning map**: this is a visual tool used in marketing to depict how consumers perceive different products, brands, or companies in relation to each other. It helps marketers understand their competitive landscape and identify opportunities for positioning their solutions effectively.

Typically, a positioning map has two axes, each representing a key attribute that is important to the target market. Common attributes include price, quality, performance, luxury, convenience, or other values (mostly reflecting some "branding elements" (see section "Branding"). The choice of axes depends on what factors are most relevant to consumer decision-making in a particular market. Once you've chosen the attributes, you can plot the existing solutions on the map, based on the gathered market data. In the end, you can decide where to plot your own solution compared to the competition trying to get a "unique" position.

Example: Positioning within the sports gear market

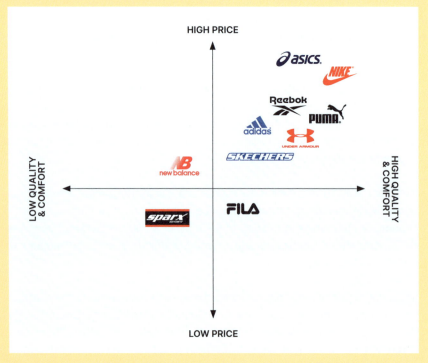

Figure 1.19: Positioning map "Sports gear" brands [27]

Looking at the positioning map above, it's very difficult to compete within this market, as almost all brands focus on the High Quality / High Price segment. The difference between each brand will come from its difference in branding.

Here's a brief overview of the branding differences between the brands:

Nike: Innovation, performance, and aspiration. Known for cutting-edge technology, elite athletes, and empowering messages ("Just Do It").

Adidas: Performance with style, sustainability, and inclusivity. Focuses on both sports and lifestyle, with eco-conscious initiatives and iconic collaborations.

Puma: Sporty style and versatility. Appeals to both athletes and fashion-conscious consumers, with a focus on creativity and collaborations with celebrities and designers.

Under Armour: High-performance and durability. Targets serious athletes with tech-driven apparel designed for maximum performance and endurance.

Asics: Comfort, precision, and support. Primarily known for running shoes with a focus on high-quality engineering and biomechanics.

Reebok: Fitness and empowerment. Emphasises health, fitness, and active lifestyle, with a strong presence in CrossFit and athleisure markets.

For a "new brand", it might be interesting to follow the FILA position as a starting point, being a High Quality / Low Price segment and evolving over time towards the higher price segment. This positioning allows the brand to attract consumers who want good quality products at an affordable price – a niche not as fiercely competitive as the premium, high-price segments.

Example: "Positioning Strategy" and its evolution:

Positioning: The new brand could position itself similarly to FILA, offering high-quality sports gear (e.g. durable, comfortable footwear, breathable apparel) at a lower price. By focusing on value for money, the brand could appeal to consumers who appreciate quality but are budget-conscious.

Brand Messaging: The messaging would emphasise affordable quality – promising performance, durability, and comfort without the high price tag of Nike or Adidas. The brand could highlight that it's a "smart choice" for consumers who want the best balance of price and performance.

Growth Path: Once the brand gains traction in the High Quality / Low Price segment, it could gradually evolve towards the High Quality / High Price segment by introducing premium products, limited-edition releases, or performance-focused innovations that allow for higher prices.

d. STP model: conclusion

Let's summarise the whole STP model process with an elaborated example for a well-known brand, Red Bull.

Example: Red Bull: the same can but a different "solution"

Figure 1.20: Red Bull can [28]

Red Bull is a well-known Austrian "energy drink", launched at the end of the 1980s, which has revolutionised the world of soft drinks.

You can look at "Red Bull" as an "energy drink"-solution, though this wouldn't explain the success of this brand. Actually, Red Bull focuses on the needs of their customer segments and adapts its strategy to those. Here's an elaborated STP model for Red Bull.

1. **Segmentation**
   Red Bull segments its market based on psychographic and behavioural factors, targeting customers with different needs and lifestyles:
   - Teenagers: This group seeks social approval and wants to appear mature in front of their peers. They are drawn to Red Bull as a drink that helps them feel grown-up and energetic.
   - Students: Students often face long study hours or social nights out. They need a quick energy boost to stay awake and focused, making Red Bull an ideal drink for studying or socialising.
   - Young Adults: These consumers balance active personal lives with

professional responsibilities. They need energy to manage fatigue and maintain performance in both work and personal activities.

2. Targeting (Differentiated Strategy)

Red Bull adopts a differentiated marketing strategy, targeting each segment with tailored messages and unique value propositions.

- Teenagers: Red Bull positions itself as the drink that boosts energy and social status. It's marketed as an exciting "adult" beverage that helps teenagers stay alert and cool among their peers.
  Example: Red Bull sponsors extreme sports and music festivals that appeal to youthful energy and social connection.
- Students: Red Bull targets students as a solution for staying energised during late-night study sessions or socialising with friends. It's marketed as the drink that helps students balance academic stress and social life.
  Example: Promotional campaigns like "Red Bull Study Breaks" and free samples on campuses emphasise focus and energy during exams.
- Young Adults: For young adults, Red Bull is positioned as a drink that helps maintain energy through a busy, demanding lifestyle – whether balancing work, personal activities, or both.
  Example: Red Bull's marketing often ties the brand to high-energy professional and athletic environments, such as sponsoring entrepreneurs and extreme sports events.

3. Positioning

Red Bull is positioned as a performance-enhancing, energy-boosting brand that helps consumers push beyond their limits. The tagline "Red Bull gives you wings" captures this promise of vitality and energy, appealing to an active, ambitious lifestyle.

Red Bull is more than just an energy drink; it's a symbol of adventure, youthful energy, and ambition. It supports consumers who are driven by both physical and mental performance, whether they're studying, working, or seeking thrills.

It's clear that all need states are different, though they might be solved by the solution "Red Bull".

2.1.6 Overview on "Solution"

a. Solution is the first element of the SAVE model and focuses around the way to respond to certain existing "customer or consumer needs".
b. These needs can be divided into several levels, explained by Maslow's model. Some need states are more important than others, creating a certain hierarchy among them. Solutions responding to "higher needs" are more valuable for consumers.
c. Each solution can be translated into different types, according to the relevant higher needs. Kotler described this in his "Five products level model".
d. "Brands" are particular examples of types of solutions: they create more trust in consumers through their emotional elements, which can be described though the models of Keller (CBBE) or Kapferer (Diamond Model).
e. Finally, the same solution might tackle different need states, depending on the type of consumer. In marketing, you will try to position your solution as closely as possible to the need of your target groups. This strategy is the three-step approach of the STP model: segmentation – targeting – positioning.

2.2 Access

2.2.1 General

Talking about "access" means explaining the different ways a customer can come into contact with the solution proposals, described in the previous section. This element from the SAVE model has evolved dramatically over the past decades. When Philip Kotler launched the idea of the 4Ps model, he could actually put every contact function under the umbrella of the (physical) P of Place, though the digitalisation of the world forced marketers to rethink the whole concept towards a more globalised idea of "access" or "accessibility".

With "access" we can explain it as the importance of being at every moment of possible connection (or touchpoint) with your customer in its total journey or relationship with your offered solution. At the centre of this "customer journey" (more information about this topic later in this book), there's a "deal"-making moment. In most of the times, this deal consists of a purchase or a sales act, though it might be

expressed under other forms such as exchange or swap, rental, free usage, ... Under these circumstances you can distinguish 3 important sections within this journey:
   a. The touchpoints **before** the deal
   b. The touchpoints to close the deal itself
   c. The touchpoints **after** the deal

Each part has its own specifics, all focusing towards an optimal "access" strategy in your customer. These will be explained in detail in the following sections.

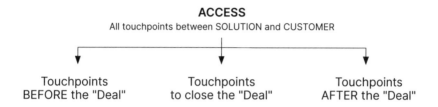

Figure 1.21: The different Access elements

2.2.1.1 Access "part 1": information

As mentioned above, customers are pursuing a certain "journey" in their search for a solution to fulfil an existing need related to a certain problem or issue (see section 2.1 Solution). All activities are focused on getting the solution ("closing the deal") and solving the problem or fulfilling this need. But before accepting the deal, they want to be reassured that the solution is worthwhile or in other words... **the proposed solution is the best value for them**.

That's why customers need "**information**" to get the reassurance to accept the deal. This information will lead to "knowledge" and "trust" to make it possible to evaluate ("e-VALUE"-ate) the proposed solution.

The information can be found from different sources:
- the customer itself (own experience)
- the communication channels of the solution
- third parties.

Chapter 2: The "evolved" model: SAVE

As marketer it is crucial to organise your activities this way, making sure that at any moment or space (potential) customers can come into contact with the necessary information. This means you need to verify that the "**accessibility**" **of the information is guaranteed**.

Which type of information to be provided during this "journey", will be described in section "Education" since the parts Access and Education are very closely linked to each other.

2.2.1.2 Access "part 2": closing the "deal"

After having evaluated all the information, customers will decide which solution gives them the perfect "value" for their need. If they decide to go for a certain proposal, there will be a "deal" between them and the provider of the solution.
In most cases, this "deal" is monetary and we can speak about purchase or sale. But there might be other ways of making a deal besides "sales", like ...

a. **Rental or lease**: customers pay to use a solution for a specified period without owning it outright.
b. **Subscription**: customers pay a regular fee to access a service or receive solutions on an ongoing basis, often monthly or annually.
c. **Licencing**: customers pay for the right to use a particular product, service, or intellectual property under certain conditions.
d. **Freemium model**: basic services are offered for free, with additional features or premium content available for a fee.
e. **Exchange**: customers may swap a product for another product.
f. Free usage or other partnerships.

In this part of "Access", the **guarantee** for the customer to close the deal is very important. Similar to part 1 (Information), you can do this offline and/or online, depending on the nature of the deal and the solution. The most often used "Access" channels for closing deals are physical shops or offices and web shops.

2.2.1.3 Access "part 3": customer service

Closing a "deal" (as described in part 2) is the beginning of a relationship between provider and customer, with certain rights or liabilities linked to the transaction. This means that you as provider want to keep "access" as optimal as possible for your customers to keep the trust in this partnership high. Most of these activities

can be put under the umbrella of "customer service":
  a. **Guarantees and help tools** on the use of the "sold" solution
  b. The **right to stop** the "deal" (e.g. right of refusal or return)
  c. Providing **extra information sources** if there are any questions from the customer.

In addition, this deal can be the perfect opportunity for marketers to grow a long-term relationship with their customers that will be the source of new future deals. We're talking about:
  a. Asking for **feedback** about and active participation to sustain the SAVE elements
  b. Keeping the relationship alive by providing "**new**" **information** (e.g. promotions, newsletters, ...)

Companies often consider the Access activities in part 3 as a cost without clear short-term return as they focus only on getting the deal done. Marketing-driven organisations know that this part is the most profitable one in the long term, as it would cost you much more to attract a new customer than to keep an existing one satisfied and broaden the relationship with them.

Comparable to part 1, all the Access activities in part 3 are closely related to the ones described in the Education section.

2.2.2 Different types of "Access channels"

We've described the different objectives of being accessible for a company with (potential) customers. It mainly comes down to 3 big parts:
  a. Part 1: providing information
  b. Part 2: closing a deal
  c. Part 3: sustaining the relationship (customer service, new information ...)

In order to optimise your access strategy, you will need to choose **the way you want to stay in contact with your customer**. This might be done in various ways:
  a. direct or indirect
  b. through online or offline channels
  c. ... and all kinds of combinations of both criteria of Access channels.[29]

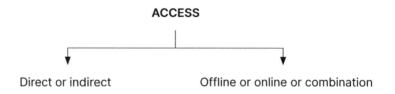

Figure 1.22: Different types of Access

Let's take a deeper dive into that matter.

- **Direct and indirect Access channels**
  Each provider of a solution proposal will need to choose the way they want to stay in contact with their customer: **direct or indirect**.
  When they choose "**direct**" access, they have a direct connection to their customers without any middleman. When the access is "**indirect**", their deal solution passes through multiple intermediaries before reaching the ultimate consumer.

  Middlemen between provider and consumer in an indirect access might be:
  a. Wholesaler
  b. Distributor
  c. Dealer
  d. Retailer
  e. Consultant
  f. Catalogue
  g. Internet

Example: Sales of wines

Figure 1.23: Sales of wine [30]

Wine distribution involves the methods and intermediaries used to get the product from the producer to the final consumer. There are two main types of access: direct and indirect.

a. **Direct Access**

In a "direct model", the wine producer or supplier sells directly to the consumer. This approach allows for a closer relationship with the customer and greater control over the branding, pricing, and customer experience. Common examples of direct access in the wine industry include wine clubs, winery tasting rooms, and online wine web shops run by producers themselves.

b. **Indirect Access**

In an "indirect model", the wine passes through multiple intermediaries before reaching the consumer. These intermediaries – also known as middlemen – include:
- Wholesalers/distributors: They purchase wine in bulk from producers and sell it to distributors, retailers, or other businesses.
- Dealers/consultants: These businesses or individuals might specialise in selling wine to particular segments, such as restaurants, hotels, or collectors.
- Retailers: Supermarkets, liquor stores, and specialised wine shops where consumers buy wine directly.

- Catalogues & Internet: Sales through mail-order catalogues or online platforms (e-commerce) that connect consumers with various wine options, often through both retailers and producers.

The way they choose can change throughout the life of their business. They may start out wanting to use only a direct channel, but as they grow they may want to change their main distribution channel focus to indirect. Or it's also possible to keep only the information part direct and to do the other parts indirectly by using intermediate parties or vice versa.

Let's focus on some advantages and disadvantages of both Access types.

- **Direct access channel**
  As mentioned above, this is a company that keeps a **direct connection** to their consumers through its communication and deal channels like direct mail of its own solutions, or its own e-commerce site. Having direct access to your customer helps keep costs down and can generally mean larger profits.

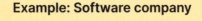

Example: Software company

Figure 1.24: Salesforce: software company CRM [31]

A software company that sells a digital product, like a CRM tool.

If the company uses a direct distribution model, they would sell the software directly to customers through their website. The business only needs to invest in the website, hosting, and online payment systems.

There's no physical shipping involved, and the product is delivered instantly via download or access keys. The company also has full control over the customer experience, including quality, updates, and support, ensuring that the software meets user expectations.

- **Indirect access channel**
  Unlike the direct access channel, indirect channels are a little more complex and involve **more third parties**. That isn't necessarily a bad thing, but it does require a little more strategic planning.

Example: FMCG

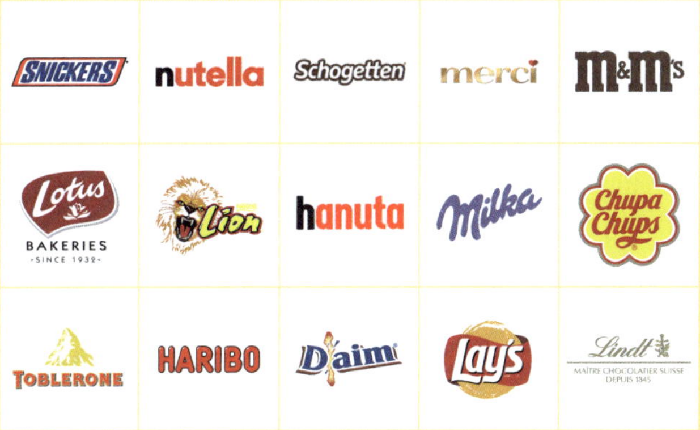

Figure 1.25: some FMCG brands [32]

A lot of fast-moving consumer goods ("FMCG") companies use a multi-tier, indirect access channel. They sell their products and brands to distributors, who sell to retailers, who sell to consumers. Most manufacturers will use the indirect access channels to sell their products on the shelves of retailers where consumers can buy them. Some of them also sell directly to consumers onsite at the manufacturing premises of their web shop.

Using both approaches, they reach a mass market through an indirect access channel and a smaller market through direct access via on-site retail operations that they own.

Larger companies who have more resources may in fact find indirect access channels to be most efficient and profitable. These third parties have their own strengths to be leveraged to reach potential customers.

One important element by using indirect access channels: **the end price** to the customer will be **higher** as every "partner" in the total access chain wants their share of the profit. So by using the indirect channels, you'll almost always have to increase the price accordingly. With direct distribution channels you can often keep the price lower compared to the indirect route.

- **Offline and online Access channels**
  Throughout this section, it's clear marketers need to maintain a close look at the touchpoints with their customers through different channels. In today's world, the channels of access might be **digital (online) and/or physical (offline)**, depending on the degree of (common) knowledge about the solution.

TYPE OF TOUCHPOINT	EXAMPLES	ADVANTAGES
ONLINE / DIGITAL	• Internet • Social Media • Smartphone applications • Virtual reality (metaverse) • Augmented reality • ...	• Getting all sorts of data which can help to tailor your solution • Endless quantities of solutions together with optimising stocks matter • Easier possibility to evaluate the different solution proposals
OFFLINE / PHYSICAL	• (Traditional) Media • Physical stores • Events • In-person / Face-to-face communication	• Creating extra visibility in a certain area / possibility to stand out of the clutter • Creating more in-depth access to customers • Better use of all human senses (stronger experiences) • Active conversations to provide the best solution to the need

Figure 1.26: Online vs offline touchpoints

It's clear, when you want to buy a loaf of bread, you won't need extensive information to make your decision, though it will be different when you want to buy a new electric car. In the latter case, you will inform yourself about the possibilities through the digital channels combined with visits to (offline) car dealers.

It all depends on the solution type and the customer profile to see which channels you need to activate to optimise your accessibility strategy. Of course, by using both types of channels (also called "Bricks and clicks" approach), you can get the best of both worlds.

2.2.3 Omni-channel

In previous sections, we described different ways of organising your Access strategy by choosing the right combination of channels, all having their own specifics and strengths. The final decision is in the hands of the provider how to structure it in order to optimise the possible relationship with your customer.

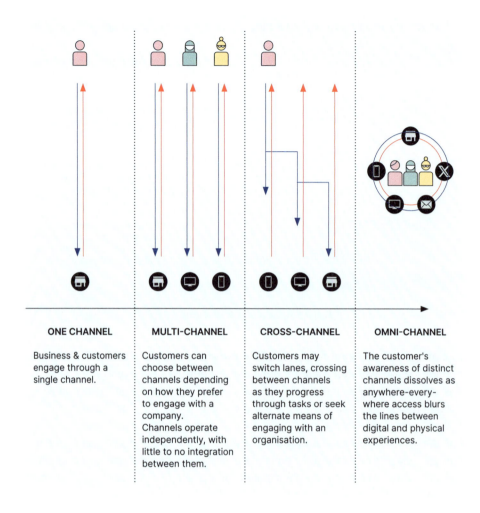

Figure 1.27: Different ways of relationship between business and customer [33]

In general you can define 4 ways of channel organisation:
a. **Single channel approach**: it focuses on one specific platform or medium to deliver products or services, allowing for a streamlined and concentrated effort.
b. **Multi-channel approach**: this way you expand the reach by incorporating multiple platforms simultaneously, catering to diverse consumer preferences. The channels operate "independently" from each other.
c. **Cross-channel approach**: cross-channel integration ensures seamless com-

munication and coordination across various channels, providing customers with a cohesive experience.
d. **Omni-channel approach**: the "ultimate" way of exploiting your Accessiblity to your customers. Throughout the journey, the "customer" remains at the heart of all touchpoints, where information and data exchange is organised at all channels at any moment in time and space, leading to the perfect customer experience both online and offline during all 3 parts of the (customer) journey.

In an omni-channel strategy, the different channels (such as brick-and-mortar stores, websites, mobile apps, social media, and more) are interconnected, allowing customers to transition effortlessly between them while maintaining a consistent and unified experience.

Example: Omni-channel for Nike running shoes

Figure 1.28: Nike running shoes & Nike Fit app [34/35]

Nike offers a seamless omni-channel experience that blends digital and physical touchpoints to create a personalised shopping journey. Customers can browse and shop on the Nike app or website, where they receive tailored product recommendations based on their purchase history and workout data (possible through the Nike Run app). They can even check product availability at nearby stores in real-time before making a decision.

For an even more personalised experience, Nike Fit technology allows customers to scan their feet at home using the Nike app. By simply placing their feet on the floor and following the app's instructions, users can get an accurate measurement of their foot size and shape. The app then suggests the best-fitting shoes based on those measurements, ensuring the right fit before purchasing.

If customers prefer to see the shoes in person, they can visit a Nike store, where sales associates have access to the same data from the app. This enables them to offer tailored product recommendations and assist in finding the best fit.

Nike also offers click-and-collect, allowing customers to order online and pick up their purchases at a nearby store, skipping shipping wait times. Plus, their loyalty programme ties everything together, letting members earn points from both in-store and online purchases and receive exclusive offers and personalised workout content through the app.

Nike's omni-channel approach ensures a smooth and integrated experience across all touchpoints – whether shopping online, in-store, or at home. It's designed to meet customers where they are, making the journey personalised, convenient, and connected.

Key elements of an **omni-channel** approach include:
a. **Unified Customer data & personalisation**: gather and centralise customer data from various touchpoints to create a 360-degree view of each customer. This data includes their preferences, purchase history, interactions, and more.
b. **Consistent messaging**: the communication ensures that marketing messages, promotions, and branding remain consistent across all channels. This consistency helps in reinforcing the brand identity and building trust with customers.
c. **Cross-channel integration**: seamless integration allows customers to start their journey on one channel and continue it on another without disruptions.
d. **Inventory and order management**: a clear synchronisation between the inventory and order management systems across all channels. This ensures that customers have access to real-time information about product availability, order status, and delivery options, regardless of the channel they choose.

e. **Customer support integration**: an omni-channel strategy extends to customer support, allowing customers to seek assistance through various channels seamlessly.

It's clear that choosing an omni-channel approach means investing in the necessary technological tools to make sure that the customer can go smoothly from one stage to another without any frictions. Besides that, it's important to keep analysing customer feedback, monitoring analytics, and adapting strategies based on emerging trends in order to remain agile and responsive to changing customer expectations and market dynamics.

2.2.4 Access channels considerations

When choosing which distribution channels are right for your business, there are many factors to consider. Remember, you can take advantage of both direct and indirect channels or offline and online channels, depending on the resources you have.

- How does the end-user like to go for these types of solutions? Does the consumer want to touch and examine the product or is it a product that the target audience likes to buy online?
- What, if any, are the local, regional, or national regulations regarding the solution category's access channels?
- Does the customer need personalised service?
- Does the solution itself need to be serviced? Or any form of installation?
- How do the competitors reach their customers?
- ...

Some extra information: Access according to Kahneman's theory

As mentioned, according to Daniel Kahneman's theory of dual-system thinking, consumers make decisions using two systems: **System 1** (fast, intuitive, and automatic) and **System 2** (slow, deliberate, and rational).

Concerning the Access case, businesses try to remain in System 1 thinking as much as possible. Consumers don't want to continuously switch from System 1 to System 2... This is why businesses want no mental barriers at all in the shopping process. This is the so-called **optimisation of the User (or Shopper) Experience (UX optimisation)**.

2.2.5 Overview on "Access"

a. Access is the second element of the SAVE model and focuses on all possible touchpoints customers may use in (starting) the relationship to get a certain "solution". Acquiring this solution can be seen as closing a "deal".
b. Access can be divided into 3 main parts:
- Touchpoints/channels before getting the deal
- Touchpoints/channels to close the deal
- Touchpoints/channels after getting the deal.
c. Each part of the Access areas has their own specificities, although they are all focused on helping the customer to pass smoothly from one area to another.
d. There are several types of channel with individual strengths (and weaknesses):
- Direct vs indirect
- Offline vs online.
e. "Omni-channel" can be considered a beautiful example of how to optimise your Access strategy to procure the best "User Experience" along the customer's journey.
- ...

2.3 Education

2.3.1 General

"**Education**" is the third pillar in your marketing mix and is very closely related to the second one, "Access". "Education" is also known as all the activities that inform the customer about the proposed solution. In the "Access" section, we discussed the channels and the touchpoints; "Education" is the information (or content) you will use in these touchpoints. That's why "Access" and "Education" work hand in hand.

Under the 4Ps model of Kotler, you can define it as "communication", "promotion" and "loyalty/repurchase" actions. "Education" can be seen as an overall term capturing all 3 elements from 4P.

In general, "Education" comes back to the following process:

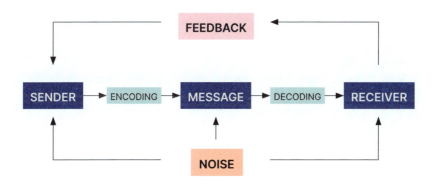

Figure 1.29: The communication-process (in general) [36]

When you think about "Education" (or communication) in its simplest form, the process is really quite linear. There's a sender of a message. The sender has an idea and puts that into words, which is encoding the message.

And then there's a recipient of a message. The message comes out of your "communication channel". It's decoded or processed by the recipient, who then decides on the meaning of your words as a result of that decoding process.

After this process, the receiver will have some feedback or will do some actions, which is relevant for the sender. Sometimes the action will be troubled with noise, as the receiver hasn't correctly decoded the message coming from the sender, which can lead to frictions between both. The sender will correct its message so that the receiver can change its meaning.

This whole process, the steps between a source and receiver that result in the transference and understanding of meaning, is called the "**communication feedback loop**". This pattern will return in every flow of "Education" between sender and receiver.

Although the "Education" possibilities have increased after the digital revolutions from the past decades, the objectives remained the same and go hand in hand with the reasoning behind the activities described under the "Access" section:
- a. Part 1: providing information
- b. Part 2: closing a deal
- c. Part 3: sustaining the relationship (customer service, new information, ...)

In part 1, "Education" can be split up into 2 major blocks with specific purposes towards customers:
- Building awareness and brand equity
- Building consideration and interest

You can consider the first block as "**communication**", where the second one is more seen as "**promotion**" or "**incentive**".

"Education" in part 2 is rather limited to information about the deal itself: terms and conditions, contract information, ...

On the other hand, the following part 3 of "Education" is very important as it consists of all actions with information leading to a perfect post-deal experience and consequently to a long-term relationship:
- From provider to customer: tutorial, newsletter, email, events, ...
- From customer to provider: feedback, reviews, ...

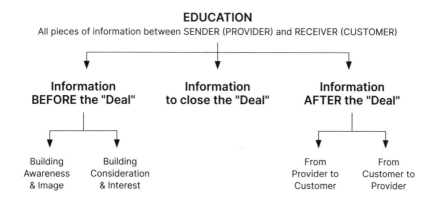

Figure 1.30: The different Access elements

Where "Access" focuses more on the digital and physical touchpoints and channels between the provider and its customer, "Education" takes care of the information ("content") between them, which reaffirms the same structure.

More details about all steps and elements will be explained further in the book (see "Customer Decision Journey").

2.3.2 PESO model

Over the past decades, the evolution of "Education" has been a dynamic process, marked by significant advancements in technology and changes in societal structures. We've experienced a clear transition **from one-way to more dialogic communication** reflecting the increasing interactivity and interconnectedness in human interactions. Due to these dynamics, the "Education" framework and more particularly the "communication" have been subjected to several changes, especially thanks to the development of digital media channels, like websites, social media, ...

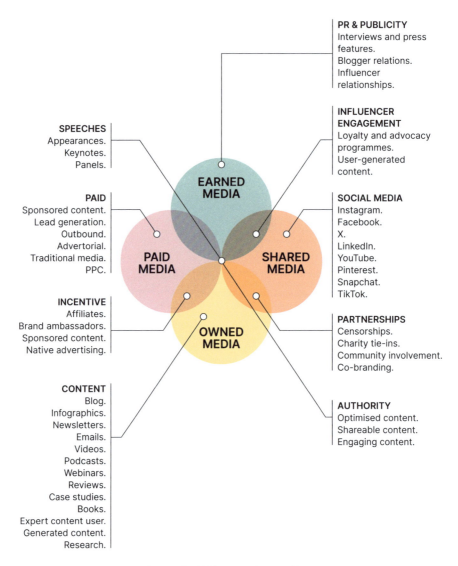

Figure 1.31: PESO media elements [38]

The **PESO model**[37] is a framework for organising and integrating different types of communication channels or media in a strategic and coordinated way. The acronym PESO stands for **Paid, Earned, Shared, and Owned media**. It was introduced by Gini Dietrich, the founder of Spin Sucks, as a way to help organisations plan and execute their communication strategies more effectively. The PESO model can be shown as follows (including certain examples):

Here's an explanation of each component of the PESO model:

a. **Paid Media**:
- Definition: paid media refers to any form of media or promotional activities that **a company pays for**. This includes traditional advertising, online advertising, sponsored content, and paid social media promotions.
- Purpose: paid media helps organisations **reach** a wider audience **quickly** and can be particularly useful for **targeting specific demographics or promoting time-sensitive content**.

b. **Earned Media**:
- Definition: earned media is **publicity or exposure** gained through efforts **other than paid** advertising. It includes media coverage, reviews, word-of-mouth recommendations, and social media mentions that are earned through the merits of the content or actions of the organisation.
- Purpose: earned media is often seen as **more credible** since it is not directly paid for by the organisation. It relies on **building positive relationships** with the audience and the media.

c. **Shared Media**:
- Definition: shared media refers to the content that is **shared** by users on **social media platforms**. This includes social media posts, retweets, shares, and other forms of user-generated content.
- Purpose: shared media leverages the power of social networks to **amplify the reach of content**. It relies on audience engagement and encourages the sharing of information within social circles.

d. **Owned media**:
- Definition: owned media refers to the communication channels that the **provider controls**. This includes the company website, blogs, newsletters, and other content that the organisation creates and manages.
- Purpose: owned media provides the organisation with **direct control over its messaging and brand image**. It is a platform for showcasing expertise, sharing company news, and building a consistent brand narrative.

By incorporating all four elements of the PESO model, organisations can create a more comprehensive and integrated communication strategy. The model recognises that successful communication is not limited to a single channel but rather requires **a strategic mix of paid, earned, shared, and owned media** to effectively engage with the target audience and achieve communication objectives.

The PESO model contains all kinds of channels and drivers that can be used for "communication" (media) or for promotional activities (incentives), which will be described in the next section.

Extra information: Influencer marketing

Influencer marketing involves collaborating with individuals who have a large and engaged number of followers on platforms like Instagram, YouTube, TikTok, or other social media channels. These influencers create content that promotes a brand's products or services, leveraging their trust and credibility with their audience. While influencer marketing spans different types of media, it primarily fits into Paid and Earned media within the PESO model.

Figure 1.32: Influencer "VEXX" [39]

1. **Paid Media**: Influencer marketing is predominantly classified under Paid media because brands compensate influencers for promoting their products. This compensation can come in the form of money, free products, or other incentives. Influencers create sponsored posts, product reviews, videos, or other content tailored to their audience. The key advantage of Paid media in influencer marketing is that it allows brands to tap into the influencer's established audience, providing access to a highly targeted and engaged group of potential customers. It also ensures that the brand's message is delivered in an authentic and trusted manner, as influencers have built credibility with their followers over time.
2. **Earned & Shared Media**: While influencer marketing is paid, it can generate Earned and Shared media when the content goes beyond the paid promotion. If an influencer's post resonates strongly with their followers, it can trigger organic engagement such as likes, shares, comments, or discussions on social media. This type of engagement is considered Earned & Shared media because it occurs without additional financial investment from the brand.

2.3.3 The difference between Communication (Media) and Promotion

Communication

As mentioned above, we consider "**communication**" as all actions done by marketing to "educate" your target group about the provided solution, which means **increasing awareness and creating a certain brand identity** around it. These are actually the first steps in the Customer Decision Journey (see next section). Communication itself also has a more long-term impact compared to promotions.

Communication is the typical playfield of brands, which are in fact complex **networks of tangible and intangible elements around the proposed solution**. These elements can be described by the branding models like CBBE (by Keller) or Diamond model/ Brand Prism (by Kapferer) (see previously). Brands will use all senses to stimulate the neurons in the brains of customers:

a. Visual (logos, names, colour, texts – humorous , erotic, emotional, ... – slogans, images, ...)

b. Audio (jingle, music, characteristic sounds, ...)
c. Smell
d. Touch
e. Taste

By combining different kinds of communication platforms with the right content, customers will be "educated" about the different solutions with both rational and emotional features (branding models). All PESO-channels can possibly lead to awareness, but **Paid (different media channels) and Earned (Word-of-mouth)** are the ones mostly used by marketers.

Promotion

Creating awareness and a certain brand image around your solution might be not enough to close the deal with your potential customer. In some cases it will be necessary to persuade them by giving a "promotion". Promotions are activities that **add short term value to convince potential customers to choose your solution**. Some examples are:
a. Price discount (e.g. −10%)
b. Volume discount (e.g. 3+1 free promotion)
c. Free sampling (e.g. free tasting)
d. Free use of the solution (e.g. test ride)
e. "No pay no cure" / "Money-back guarantee"
f. Free services (e.g. free delivery when purchasing on web shop)

To communicate promotions, you can use the **same media channels** as those to build awareness (see previous chapter), though the content will be more focused around the **short-term value**. They will use more direct channels with **quick customer response**. That's why promotions are the perfect tool of Education during the last stages of part 1 – trying to convince target customers to choose the solution.

MARKETING COMMUNICATION	MARKETING PROMOTION
Brand strategy for brand buiilding and awareness.	Focused tactics for immediate sales boost.
Includes wider activities like relations and Mobile Marketing Communication.	Sepcific tactics like discounts and special offers.
Aims for long-term customer relationships.	Targets short-term sales goals.
Utilises various channels, including Visual Merchandising Communication in Marketing.	Direct marketing techniques for quick consumer response.
Measures success through brand equity and customer loyalty.	Measured by sales volume and campaign ROI.
Storytelling to connect emotionally with the audience.	Persuasive calls to action for immediate puchase.

Figure 1.33: Communication vs promotion [40]

2.3.4 Content marketing: 3H model of Google

Education is the basics of marketing – trying to convince customers to go for your solution. As a marketer, besides deciding which possible channels you will use to reach your customers, you also need to be aware of the type of message you want to convey to them, which comes down to deciding what **type of content** is suitable.

Based on massive research that Google performed some years ago on how people use YouTube, they came up with a model called "3H": the "Hero, Hub, and Hygiene" content strategy model.

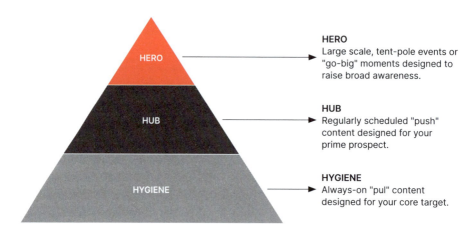

Figure 1.34: 3H model by Google [41]

This model is often used in (digital) marketing and content creation to organise and **categorise content based on its purpose and audience engagement**. Let's break down each component:
1. **Hero content**
   - Purpose: Hero content is designed to make a significant impact and generate high visibility (**building awareness**). It often involves large-scale campaigns, events, or major releases.
   - Frequency: Typically, hero content is produced **less frequently**, often as a flagship or flagship series.

2. **Hub content**
   - Purpose: Hub content aims to engage and maintain a consistent audience. It's focused **on building a loyal viewership and is often episodic or thematic**.
   - Frequency: Hub content is produced **more regularly** than hero content but less frequently than hygiene content.
3. **Hygiene (or Help) content**
   - Purpose: Hygiene content addresses the audience's **basic needs and concerns**. It's the day-to-day content that helps maintain and grow the overall audience. **It's the type of content customers are searching for**.
   - Frequency: Hygiene content is produced regularly and consistently, addressing ongoing needs and questions.

This model helps content creators and marketers create a balanced and effective content strategy. By combining these three types of content, you can attract new audiences (hero), keep existing audiences engaged (hub), and address ongoing needs (hygiene).

Example: The 3H model for Coca-Cola

Figure 1.35: Share the magic, and Coke & Food pairings [42/43]

1. **HERO Content: Big, Brand-Building Moments**
   Objective: Coca-Cola's Hero content creates large-scale brand awareness and celebrates universal moments of joy and togetherness. It's about telling emotionally impactful stories that connect with people globally.
   Content Example: For the holidays, Coca-Cola could release a cinematic "Share the Magic" commercial, building on the brand's iconic holiday trucks and featuring diverse families and communities coming together

over a Coke, spreading happiness. The ad would focus on the warmth of shared experiences and be visually striking, with heartwarming music and imagery that evokes nostalgia and joy.

Distribution: This content would air across TV, YouTube, Instagram, and during major global events like the Super Bowl or the Olympics.

2. HUB Content: Regular Engagement with Fans

Objective: Hub content keeps Coca-Cola top of mind, offering ongoing engagement with the brand's community. It focuses on brand affinity, product usage, and building deeper connections.

Content Example: A "Coke & Food Pairings" video series on social media, where each episode highlights fun and surprising food combinations with Coca-Cola. Episodes could feature influencers and chefs creating unique meals paired with different Coca-Cola beverages, inviting fans to share their own pairings.

Distribution: Weekly posts on Instagram, YouTube, and TikTok, supported by influencer collaborations.

3. HYGIENE Content: Practical, Value-Driven Content

Objective: Hygiene content serves as useful, easy-to-consume content that answers customer questions and adds value to their lives. It's about assisting the audience with practical information while reinforcing the brand's relevance.

Content Example: A "Refreshing Recipes with Coke" blog and video series, providing quick, creative ways to use Coca-Cola in cooking (e.g. Coca-Cola glazed ribs, Coke float recipes). This content offers helpful tips and inspires new ways to enjoy the product.

Distribution: Shared on Coca-Cola's website, YouTube, and through social media channels like Pinterest, where people look for recipe inspiration.

The 3H model is the basis for the so called "heartbeat" approach to planning company communications, as depicted in the chart below: a constant "hum" of the Hygiene and Hub activities, punctuated by the occasional Hero bursts. As a solution provider you will have to make sure that all 3 content types are captured in your content plan.

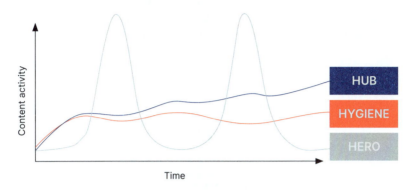

Figure 1.36: The "heartbeat" content model (based on Google's 3H framework) [44]

Referring back to the PESO model, Hero content is effective through Paid and Earned media, which means that the budgets are relatively considerable. Hub content is mostly spread through Earned and Shared media channels and needs less money. The lowest budgets are needed for Hygiene content, as it's mostly used on Owned and Shared media channels.

2.3.5 Experience marketing

2.3.5.1 General

Experiences serve as an important Education marketing tool because they create **memorable and emotional connections between brands and consumers**. Unlike traditional advertising, which often relies on one-way communication, experiential marketing engages customers in immersive, interactive, and personalised ways. This approach fosters a deeper sense of loyalty and trust as consumers feel more valued and understood. Moreover, in the digital age, these experiences are frequently shared on social media, amplifying their reach and impact far beyond the initial audience.

2.3.5.2 Model of Pine and Gilmore

Joseph Pine II and James Gilmore emphasised the strengths of experiences by developing a model, also known as the **Experience Economy**.[45] This model proposes that businesses should focus on creating memorable experiences for their customers rather than just offering goods (or brands) and services.

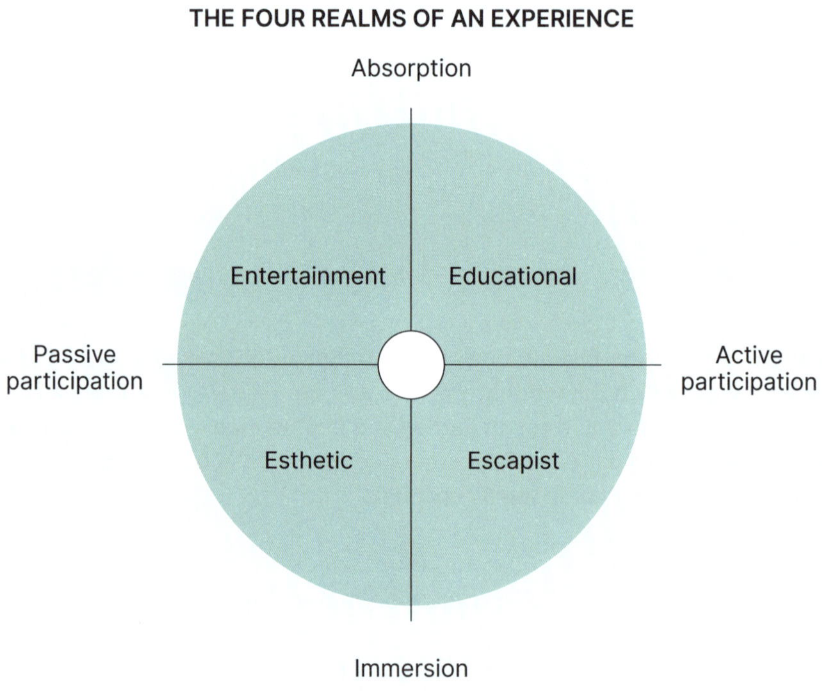

THE FOUR REALMS OF AN EXPERIENCE

Absorption

Entertainment | Educational

Passive participation — Active participation

Esthetic | Escapist

Immersion

Figure 1.37: Experience Economy (based on Pine and Gilmore) [46]

The model highlights **four dimensions of an experience**:

1. **Entertainment**: This realm involves **passive absorption** of experiences through the senses, such as watching a movie, attending a concert, or viewing a play. The customer is entertained and engaged through observation.
2. **Education**: In the educational realm, customers are more **actively** involved.

This can include participating in a workshop, attending a class, or engaging in a training session. The aim is to enrich the customer's knowledge or skills, providing value through learning.
3. **Escapism**: This realm **immerses the customer in an experience** where they **actively participate** in a different reality. Examples include playing video games, engaging in virtual reality, or taking part in adventure tourism. Customers are deeply involved and often physically and emotionally engaged.
4. **Esthetic**: This realm involves **passive immersion in an environment** where the customer is deeply involved in appreciating the setting. Examples include visiting an art gallery, touring a beautifully designed garden, or staying at a luxury resort. The focus is on creating a pleasing, memorable environment that the customer can enjoy.

> ### Example: Pine and Gilmore with some examples ...
>
> In the Experience Economy, businesses engage customers through distinct experiences that go beyond just products or services. Pine and Gilmore identify four key types of experiences:
>
> a. Entertainment:
>
>
>
> Figure 1.38: Entertainment experience [47]
>
> Watching a Netflix series at home is a perfect example. It's an immersive experience where viewers are entertained and emotionally engaged without

Chapter 2: The "evolved" model: SAVE

active participation. The experience captivates with storytelling, visuals, and characters, offering relaxation and enjoyment.

b. **Educational:**

Figure 1.39: Educational experience [48]

A cocktail or wine-tasting workshop offers a learning experience. Participants are actively involved, gaining new skills or knowledge while interacting with experts and peers. It's both informative and enriching, helping individuals develop a deeper appreciation for their craft.

c. **Escapist:**

Figure 1.40: Escapist experience [49]

Backpacking through South America exemplifies escapism. It's a fully immersive experience that allows individuals to disconnect from everyday life, offering adventure, freedom, and discovery in unfamiliar surroundings. It creates lasting memories through personal exploration.

d. Esthetic:

Figure 1.41: Esthetic experience [50]

Watching a football match at Anfield with Liverpool FC is an esthetic experience. It's about the environment – the energy of the crowd, the iconic stadium, and the live atmosphere that makes the event unforgettable. The focus here is on the sensory experience, the beauty of the moment, and the connection to something greater.

Pine and Gilmore argue that businesses can gain a competitive advantage by staging experiences that connect with customers on an emotional and personal level. The progression of economic value outlined by the authors suggests that **experiences are more valuable and differentiated than commodities, goods, or services**.

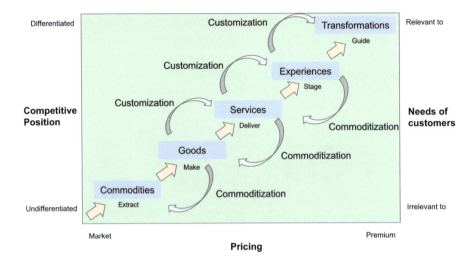

Figure 1.42: "Experiences" as part of value-optimisation [51]

The more a company or brand tries to engage their consumers through well-thought-out experiences, the higher the value they provide to their consumers. This can be achieved by a higher degree of personalisation/customisation.
The key elements of Pine and Gilmore's model include:
- **Personalisation**: Tailoring the experience to individual customer preferences and needs.
- **Engagement**: Ensuring that customers are actively involved and emotionally connected to the experience.
- **Memorability**: Creating a lasting impression that customers remember long after the experience is over.

Extra information: Experiences according to Kahneman

In his work on the Experience and Memory model, Daniel Kahneman focuses on how people perceive and remember experiences. According to Kahneman, we experience events through **two distinct "selves"**: the experiencing self (the part of us that lives through the moment) and the remembering self (the part that recalls and evaluates experiences afterwards).

One key insight from Kahneman's model is the concept of the "**peak-end rule**".

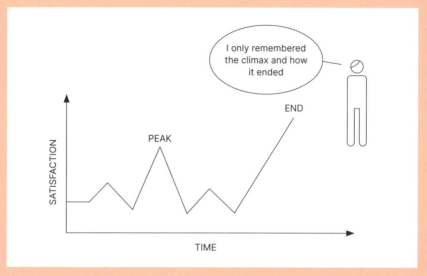

Figure 1.43: Peak-End rule by Kahneman [52]

This principle suggests that we tend to remember an experience based on its most intense moment (**the "peak"**) **and how it ends**, rather than the experience as a whole. In addition, he highlights the "duration neglect" – the idea that the length of an experience matters less than its most intense moment and final impression.

For example, if you go to a concert and the performance is fantastic but the total atmosphere is even more electrifying (the "peak"), and the event ends with a pleasant, smooth closing (the "end"), you're likely to remember it as a great experience – even if there were some boring moments in between.

In short, Kahneman's model shows that our memories of experiences are shaped more by their most extreme moments and how they end, rather than by their entire duration.

2.3.5.3 Experiences in a "digital" context

In the digital era, delivering great customer (user) experiences is crucial for successful marketing. Here are some great "experience" executions that create "trust":

    a. A seamless, user-friendly website or app design enhances customer satisfaction by providing **easy navigation and quick access** to information.

    b. Personalisation algorithms can tailor content and recommendations to individual preferences, creating a **more engaging and relevant interaction**.

    c. Robust customer support through chatbots and social media ensures **timely assistance and builds trust**.

    d. **Integrating feedback mechanisms** allows brands to continuously improve and adapt to customer needs.

These digital strategies not only enhance the customer journey but also foster loyalty and drive long-term business growth by making each interaction meaningful and memorable.

2.3.6 Overview on "Education"

    a. Education is the third element of the SAVE model and focuses on the content you will use on the Access touchpoints to convince customers to get a certain "solution". Acquiring this solution can be seen as closing a "deal". Education goes hand in hand with the Access strategy.

    b. Similar to Access, Education can be divided into 3 main parts:
- Content before a customer gets the deal
- Content related to the close of the deal
- Content after a customer gets the deal.

    c. Each part of Education, has its own specificities:
- In the first part, we can distinguish 2 main types of content: "communication", focusing more long term on brand awareness and brand image and "promotion", trying to convince the customer to take short-term action.
- In the second part, the content is more focused on certain terms and conditions.
- In the last part, the content has the objective of strengthening the relationship between "solution" and its customer. There's also a shift from one-way to a dialogue.

    d. The content (and Education activities) is spread across different media channels. We can distinguish 4 different types: Paid, Earned, Shared, and Owned

media ("PESO").
e. You can structure your content based on the types of media channels used, but you can also look at the objectives you would like to reach. This can be captured by the 3H model: by building up your (yearly) content plan into 3 sections, being Hero – Hub – Hygiene/Help, you can leverage your Education investments efficiently.
f. Experiences are special Education tools as they procure the customers some unforgettable memories of a brand. Through the model of Pine & Gilmore you can classify the different types of experiences according to certain parameters. Each type has its own objective.

2.4 Value

2.4.1 Elements of Value

Value is the last element of the SAVE model you can influence as marketer. From the customer's point of view, value is perhaps the most important pillar within the SAVE model, though it's the most difficult one for the marketer as "Value" can be considered to be the result of the actions performed under the 3 other blocks "Solution", "Access", and "Education". If your "Solution" is solving the highest needs, very easily "Accessible" and broadly and clearly known and recommended by your (target) group (aka "Education"), it will be considered the best option on the market ... procuring the highest "Value".

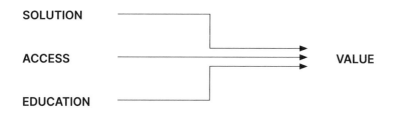

Figure 1.44: S, A and E influence V

Being driven by the other 3, maximising "Value" as such isn't easy to achieve and is subjective amongst customers. **"Value" can increase and decrease very easily as soon as the situation in the market changes due to evolving activities on the other 3 drivers**. So, as a provider it's important to closely monitor your "Value" in the market compared to the one from competitors. Let's analyse each element of Value in more detail.

2.4.1.1 Element 1 of Value: Solution

As mentioned above, Solution is all about the **needs** you would like to tackle at the customer's level. Your customer has a (potential) problem/pain which needs to be solved. Solution is the element that comes very close to a standard law in economics: **the law of supply and demand**, which will lead to the optimal "**price**".

The law of supply and demand is a fundamental principle in economics that describes the relationship between the availability of a good or service (**supply**) and the desire for that good or service (**demand**). In simple terms, the law states that the price of a product or service will tend to move towards a point where the quantity supplied equals the quantity demanded. When demand exceeds supply, prices typically rise, and when supply exceeds demand, prices generally fall. This dynamic interaction helps determine market equilibrium, where the forces of supply and demand are balanced.

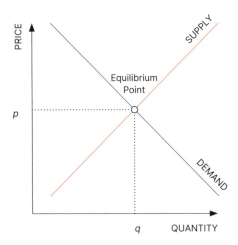

Figure 1.45: Law of supply and demand [53]

The solution in the SAVE model can be seen as the "supply" element in the law, where the need or pain of your customer is closely related to the "demand" element. As a marketer, you need to analyse the context your "Solution" taps into. In addition, you need to make sure that it's the most "unique" proposition.

You can define "**uniqueness**" in 2 ways:
a. **From the supply side**: make sure there are no "alternatives" to your "Solution" available in the market. "No competition" means "lower supply" which will lead to a higher "equilibrium price" (or "Value").
b. **From the demand side**: make sure that your "Solution" focuses on a higher need (Maslow) and/or a very clear pain/problem from the customer side. The higher the "need" and/or the more obvious the problem means "higher demand" which will lead to a higher "equilibrium price" (or "Value").

Knowing this, it's clear that "Value" is correlated to the "price" equilibrium in this economic law.

Example: The law of "supply" and "demand"... a bottle of water

Figure 1.46: A bottle of water as a "value" element [54]

Situation A: playing on the "supply" side
A bottle of water in Western countries has a "lower" Value than the same bottle of water in the Sahara desert. It's clear that in the first scenario there

are a lot of alternatives on the market for a customer, but if you're in the desert and you're thirsty, you might give everything you own to get that bottle. The "Solution" is not the same in different contexts.

Situation B: playing on the "demand" side
That same bottle of water can be provided in standard PET or in recycled PET packagings. The second proposal will be "valued" as higher as it's tapping into the need for "safety and security" on the Maslow pyramid (like all "more sustainable" solutions) and may have a higher price.

2.4.1.2 Element 2 of Value: Access

As described in the section above, the "Access" concept contains all organised activities to provide a smooth and convenient flow to customers in getting a deal and the use of it. We distinguish 3 important Access objectives:
a. Providing information
b. Closing the deal
c. Sustaining the relationship (service, ...)

As described in the introduction of this section, human beings are "lazy" and want to use their brains as little as possible by going for the System 1 "fast thinking" method. Any possible barrier might force humans to opt for System 2 and this takes mental energy, which is not optimal. As a marketer, you will therefore make your activities as "accessible" as possible by making it very "easy" or "convenient" for your customer to pass all steps. This means:
a. Providing the right information at any space or moment
b. Making the deal easily accessible and adapted to their personal needs
c. Ensuring the necessary service elements when the customer has chosen you.

The "easier" the customer goes from steps 1 to 2 to 3, the higher the "Value" they will provide to your proposal. Depending on the market context you can monetise this higher value by asking a higher price for your offer.

Example: Printer companies... HP Instant Ink

Figure 1.47: Ink cartridges [55]

Many printer companies, such as HP Instant Ink, now offer subscription-based models that simplify the printing process and deliver greater convenience to customers.

1. **Providing the right information**
   When customers visit the website, they immediately see clear information about subscription plans, such as the benefits of automatic ink delivery and potential savings. Customers can also use a print volume estimator to choose the right plan based on their monthly printing needs, and view videos or FAQs that explain how the service works. This ensures they have all the information they need to make an informed decision without any confusion.

2. **Personalised, convenient offers**
   Once the customer decides to purchase, they can select from a variety of subscription plans tailored to different printing volumes, such as 100, 300, or 500 pages per month. Pricing is transparent, with options to pay monthly or save by committing to longer terms. New customers might also receive an introductory discount or free trial, lowering the barrier to entry and increasing the chances of conversion.

3. **Effortless ongoing service**
   After subscribing, the ink is automatically delivered when the printer sig-

nals that it's running low. Customers receive usage updates to track their ink levels and can easily adjust their subscription plan if their printing needs change. The service includes customer support for any questions, ensuring a smooth experience from start to finish. If a customer decides to upgrade to a higher plan, they can do so with just a few clicks.

This subscription model provides convenience, personalisation, and savings, which makes it feel like a premium offering compared to traditional "buy-as-you-go" models. Customers appreciate the hassle-free service, leading to higher retention rates.

2.4.1.3 Element 3 of Value: Education

The last way to enhance "Value" around your proposition is by investing in "Education" tools. We described this part of SAVE as everything marketers do about communicating and promoting their solutions through different channels, covered under the PESO model. Moreover the "Education" flow goes hand in hand with "Access" opportunities and customers want to experience the same level of "easiness" in the communication and promotion activities as in those of "Access". As marketer, you need to master your "Education" activities, which means...

a. Build your story by creating the **right content following the 3H model**.
b. Distribute this content towards your target customers by **managing the different communication channels (PESO)**.

The more easily you can inspire your customer into this "Education", the higher the "Value" the customer will give to your solution. Moreover, certain channels of PESO are more "**trustworthy**" than others. According to marketing researchers AC Nielsen, the recommendations from people I know can be considered the most trustworthy, followed by branded websites and editorial content. Paid media (ads) are the least trustworthy information channels.

TRUST IS HIGHEST IN DEVELOPING REGIONS

PERCENT OF RESPONDENTS WHO COMPLETELY OR SOMEWHAT TRUST ADVERTISING FORMAT BY REGION

	Asia Pacific	Europe	Africa / Middle East	Latin America	North America
Recommendations from Europe I know	85%	78%	85%	88%	82%
Branded websites	78%	54%	76%	75%	61%
Editorial content, such as newspaper articles	71%	52%	71%	74%	63%
Consumer opinion posted online	70%	60%	71%	63%	66%
Ads on tv	68%	45%	70%	72%	63%
Brand sponsorships	67%	43%	73%	70%	57%
Ads in newspapers	63%	44%	69%	72%	65%
Ads in magazines	62%	43%	65%	70%	62%
Billboards and other outdoor advertising	60%	40%	64%	63%	57%
Emails I signed up for	60%	41%	59%	65%	64%
TV programme product placements	60%	35%	64%	64%	53%
Ads before movies	59%	38%	57%	62%	56%
Ads on radio	54%	41%	62%	68%	60%
Online video ads	53%	33%	55%	52%	47%
Ads on mobile devices	50%	26%	49%	48%	39%
Ads on social networks	50%	32%	57%	54%	42%
Ads served in search engine results	50%	36%	52%	58%	49%
Online banner ads	48%	27%	49%	46%	41%
Text ads on mobile devices	42%	22%	41%	39%	37%

Figure 1.48: Level of "trust" of media channels (AC Nielsen) [56]

So "**Shared**" media have the highest level of trust (and "Value"), followed by "**Owned**" and "**Earned**" media. It's clear that "**Paid**" media have the lowest "Value".

Chapter 2: The "evolved" model: SAVE

95

This result was confirmed by an academic study done in 2016 by Macnamara, explaining that the PESO model will shift further towards **SOEP**, based on the value and trust customers ascribe to the various types of media.

Although "Paid" media have the lowest level of trust and "Value", they still have an important role to play in marketing plans. More about this will be detailed in the coming sections of "Customer (Decision) Journey".

Example: User-generated content (UGC)

User-generated content (UGC) refers to any content – such as videos, photos, reviews, or social media posts – created by customers or users rather than the brand itself. UGC is valuable because it provides authentic, relatable content that can influence others' purchasing decisions and build trust in a brand.

Figure 1.49: User-generated content (UGC) by GoPro [57]

A great example of UGC is GoPro. The brand encourages its customers to share videos of their adventures using GoPro cameras, often with the hashtag #GoPro. These videos, showcasing everything from skydiving to surfing, are shared on social media and repurposed by GoPro in its marketing campaigns. This content feels genuine and helps the brand connect with its audience, showing real people using the product in exciting, everyday situations. UGC like this builds trust and authenticity, leading to greater brand awareness and customer loyalty.

2.4.2 Price-paradox

Let's close the SAVE chapter by referring back to Kotler's traditional marketing mix model: the "4P" model. Regarding "price", certain sources claim it's the most important element in your marketing plan as it will affect consumer confidence in the benefits your product or service provides. On the other hand, if you consider it as "Value", it might be the factor that is the result of the activities valued by the other 3 pillars. "**Price**" **can be both important and not important at the same time**, which could be seen as a sort of paradox.

The importance of the price element in the marketing mix can vary depending on various factors such as the industry, product type, target market, and overall marketing strategy. Here are a few considerations that might explain the seeming paradox:

a. **Product Differentiation**: In some industries, products are highly differentiated, and consumers are willing to pay premium prices for unique features or brand value. In such cases, the price becomes crucial in conveying its perceived value.

b. **Commodity Products**: On the other hand, for commodity products (like vegetables) where there is little differentiation, price might be a more critical factor in influencing consumer decisions. In this scenario, consumers may be less concerned with brand loyalty and more focused on obtaining the best deal.

c. **Target Market**: The importance of price can vary among different consumer segments. Some consumers may be highly price-sensitive, while others may prioritise quality, brand, or convenience over price.

d. **Economic Conditions**: Economic factors, such as inflation, recession, or changes in consumer income levels, can influence the significance of pricing in a particular market or industry.

e. Marketing Strategy: A company's overall marketing strategy and positioning can also impact the role of price. For example, a company may choose to compete on price to gain market share, or it may position itself as a premium brand with higher prices to convey exclusivity.

Price might be important if you consider purely economic and financial transactions between a provider and a customer, though doing business can be broader than that.

Example: Google and "price"

Figure 1.50: Google [58]

Google is one of the top 3 biggest companies in the world, though they don't ask a price for their "solutions": customers can use the services of Google free of charge, though businesses need to pay if they want to advertise through Google channels. As such, Google has chosen a complete different business model than traditional companies with great success. It's clear that the "Value" of Google is very high for both customers and businesses, although "price" is irrelevant.

In summary, price is often considered the most important factor in marketing when customers are highly price-sensitive or when the product or service is seen as a commodity, meaning it lacks distinct differentiation from competitors. In such cases, consumers tend to focus on getting the best deal or the lowest price, and price becomes the key driver of purchasing decisions.

However, while price might dominate in these situations, it is usually just one element of the larger value equation. **Value** in marketing is a broader concept, encompassing not only price but also other factors like product quality, brand reputation, convenience, customer service, and the overall experience. For instance, a consumer might be willing to pay a higher price for a premium product if it offers superior quality, unique features, or a strong brand identity that resonates with them.

Ultimately, while price can be a decisive factor, value is what creates lasting customer loyalty. By offering a combination of competitive pricing along with enhanced quality, convenience, or emotional appeal, brands can deliver a higher perceived value, which leads to greater customer satisfaction and long-term success. The focus on value – rather than just price – helps companies build stronger brand equity and justify a higher price point when appropriate.

2.4.3 Overview on "Value"

a. Value is the last element of the SAVE model and it reflects the way customers "evaluate" the different solutions, their promises and services and their feedback from others. Value is actually the pillar that is the end result of the previous other factors of SAVE.
b. Each element (S, A and E) has its own impact on the total Value part:
  - "Solution" will follow the economic law of supply and demand to a greater extent. The supply side will be covered by the number of alternatives that might exist, whereas the demand side will be impacted by the type of Maslow need the solution is aiming for.
  - "Access" is all about how smoothly and easily a customer goes through the journey flow in acquiring knowledge, closing the deal, and enjoying after-sales service.
  - And finally, "Education" goes hand in hand with the Access activities and will look after the "trust" customers will have for the offered "Solution", based on the existing content on the different PESO channels.
c. Value is more than just "price", which played a considerable part in the former 4Ps model of Kotler. It takes into account other elements from S, A and E information, like brand experience, trust, convenience, and much more.

Chapter 2: The "evolved" model: SAVE

Chapter 3:
Customer (Decision) Journey

3.1 History and trends

Marketing has always played an important role in modern civilisation, though it really became one of the crucial pillars of our economic world after some important "**revolutions**":

a. The "Industrial Revolution" reorganised the production methods on efficiency, leading to an expansion in supply and innovation.
b. The economic growth after World War II and more particularly in the 1960s boosted the demand for products, brands, and services resulting in the start of "consumerism".
c. The "first digital revolution", with the creation of the interconnected www-platforms, created possibilities for consumers to communicate and interact with their brands and services.
d. Thanks to social media and smartphone technology, we entered the era of the "second digital revolution", providing consumers with a place behind the steering wheel of communication and innovation processes.
e. And... what about AI? We are experiencing a new digital revolution at the moment...

Parallel to these "revolutions", we clearly notice the steep development of marketing as a science trying to get the necessary insights to frame it all. In the beginning marketing was more a commercial tool to influence the standard equation of supply and demand, though the more customers and brands take over the relay, the more marketing is seen as a "psychological" tool to understand consumer behaviour. The concept of the **Customer Decision Journey** ("**CDJ**") was born. It's the process that a consumer goes through from initial awareness of a product or service (solution) over the decision to make the purchase/deal to the final experience activities. This journey is often conceptualised as a series of stages that customers move through. Understanding the customer decision journey helps businesses tailor their marketing strategies to meet customer needs at each stage of the process.

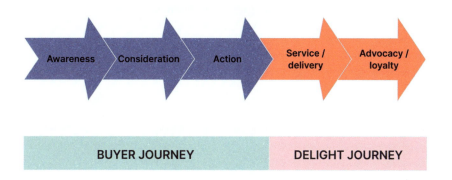

Figure 1.51: Customer Decision Journey [59]

One element takes a crucial role in all evolutionary steps: the importance of "data" to acquire the necessary knowledge of why customers are taking certain steps. In the beginning this "**data**" gathering was done through intensive analogue research. When we entered the digital era, new technologies gave us more possibilities for coping with huge amounts of data, which lead to new tools to describe this CDJ idea.

3.2 AIDA: the start

We want to start our journey with the **AIDA** model, introduced by E. St. Elmo Lewis, an American advertising and sales pioneer. While the exact date of its creation is not precisely documented, it is generally believed to have originated in the late 19th or early 20th century.

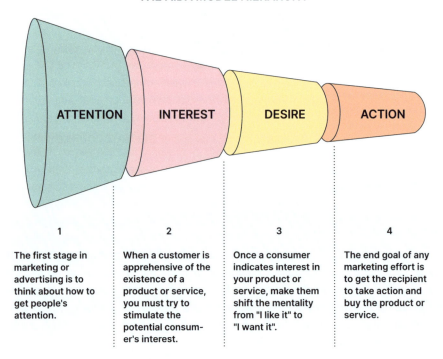

Figure 1.52: AIDA model [60]

AIDA is a classic marketing model that outlines the stages a customer goes through in the process of making a purchase decision. The acronym stands for **Attention, Interest, Desire, and Action**.

    a. **Attention**: The first step is to grab the audience's attention. In this stage, marketers aim to create awareness and make customers notice their solution. This could be achieved through compelling headlines, eye-catching visuals, or creative advertising methods that stand out in a crowded marketplace.

    b. **Interest**: Once attention is captured, the goal is to generate interest and curiosity about the solution. Marketers provide more information, highlight unique features, and emphasise benefits to keep the audience engaged.

This stage aims to make the audience want to learn more.

c. **Desire**: Having gained the audience's interest, the next step is to cultivate a desire for the product or service. Marketers focus on creating an emotional connection and showcasing how the solution addresses the customer's needs or desires. Testimonials, case studies, and persuasive content like promotions are often used to build desire.

d. **Action**: The ultimate objective of the AIDA model is to prompt the audience to take action, typically to make a purchase. Marketers provide a clear and compelling call-to-action, guiding the audience on what steps to take to acquire the solution. This could involve making a purchase online, visiting a store, or contacting the company.

The AIDA model has been widely used for decades in advertising and communication strategies, particularly in traditional advertising formats such as print, radio, and television. However, it's important to note that this journey has become more complex in the digital age, with customers often engaging in extensive online research and relying on various channels before making a purchase. While the AIDA model provides a foundational understanding of consumer behaviour, marketers may also consider more contemporary frameworks that incorporate digital influences.

3.3 The evolution in the CDJ models

It's clear that the AIDA model does not cover all aspects of total consumer behaviour: for example, it doesn't take into consideration any of the activities that occur after the purchase. Moreover, the increased grade of digitalisation changed the idea of the journey leading to new marketing models around it.

Based on empirical research, in 2009, **McKinsey & Company** suggested a dramatic alternative customer journey model to the traditional purchase funnel. Their research was founded on interviews with 20,000 businesses in the USA, Germany, and Japan.[61] They recommended a loop model instead of the usual straight-line approach from awareness, purchase, and loyalty. This was a dramatic change although, years later, many companies still work in the usual linear approach in a non-linear world.

Chapter 3: Customer (Decision) Journey 103

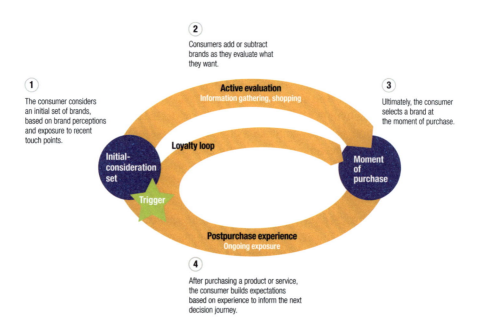

Figure 1.53: Customer Decision Journey by McKinsey & Company

The model starts on the left at the "Initial consideration set": the consumer is confronted with a certain need and wants to solve it. They will start with the solutions they were exposed to at different touchpoints or the ones they know already. This is the first phase of the journey. Thereafter they will evaluate the different options and will choose the optimal one (phase 2). The actual acquisition or the moment of purchase is captured in phase 3. After having purchased the solution, the consumer will build new expectations based on their experience of it (phase 4), hopefully leading to more loyalty actions in the future. In addition, these expectations might be the start of new journeys as they might "trigger" (see "star" sign on the model in Figure 1.53) for new consumers to start their journey. This so-called "word of mouth" can be positive or negative, in parallel to the existing experience, which might be evaluated as "good" or "bad".

Another example of a modern Customer Decision Journey model is elaborated by **Joseph Jaffe** in his book *Flip the Funnel: How to Use Existing Customers to Gain New Ones*,[62] which suggests a fundamental shift in marketing strategy. Instead of focusing primarily on acquiring new customers (AIDA), the model emphasises the importance of nurturing and retaining existing customers to drive growth and acquisition.

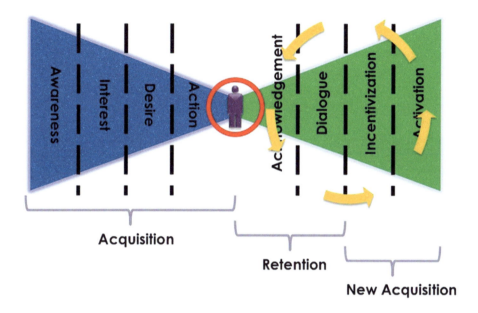

Figure 1.54: Flip the funnel (by Jaffe)

The "**Flip the funnel**" **model** consists of the 4 first stages of the AIDA model (Awareness – Interest – Desire – Action) and adds 4 more stages after the decision of "deal" described by a "flipped" abbreviation from AIDA, being ADIA (Acknowledgement – Dialogue – Incentivisation – Activation).

Jaffe argues that "At some point we're going to run out of customers, we have to keep customers so we don't have to always go looking for new ones." **It is important to use existing customers to attract new ones**. Existing customers are seen as valuable assets who have already demonstrated interest in the brand by accepting the deal (purchase). By nurturing these relationships and providing excellent customer experiences, businesses can foster loyalty, increase retention rates, and encourage repeat purchases. Also, satisfied customers can become powerful advocates for a brand. Through positive word-of-mouth recommendations, referrals, and social sharing, they can help attract new customers more effectively than traditional marketing efforts.

According to Jaffe, there are 4 key steps you need to do as marketer once a consumer has decided to go for your solution. This will lead to customer retention and help gain new acquisitions:

a. **Acknowledgement**: This stage involves recognising and acknowledging the value of existing customers. It's about demonstrating **appreciation for the purchasing act**. Acknowledgement can take various forms, such as personalised thank-you messages, exclusive offers or rewards for being a loyal customer.

b. **Dialogue**: This refers to the two-way communication between the brand and its customers. It's about actively listening to customer feedback, addressing their concerns, and engaging in meaningful conversations. Through channels like social media, email, surveys or customer service interactions, companies can gather insights into customer preferences, needs and pain points. By having an open dialogue, businesses can strengthen their understanding of their audience and tailor their offerings to better meet their expectations.

c. **Incentivisation**: Companies incentivise existing customers to start spreading the value of the brand amongst their peers. This can involve offering rewards, discounts or other exclusive value in exchange for referrals, reviews, or social media shares. By providing incentives for customers to spread positive word-of-mouth and recommend the brand to their networks, companies can leverage the power of advocacy to attract new customers more effectively.

d. **Activation**: In this last stage, existing customers take action as real advocates for the brand. This group of customers instinctively creates "content" on their own, which will be spread to the world. By activating their networks and advocating for the brand, existing customers play a vital role in driving new customer acquisition and expanding the brand's reach.

Several studies have proven it's **much more expensive to attract new customers than to retain the existing ones**. Joseph Jaffe defends this philosophy through his model, by recommending that brands focus on getting a closer relationship with their customers. The ultimate dream of each brand is the creation of so-called "brand communities" in which brand ambassadors share their experiences with each other and convince new customers to choose it.

It's clear that this idea – the Customer Decision Journey – made huge steps forward once data-driven businesses took the lead in the marketing world. The biggest companies of today, like Google, Meta, Microsoft, Apple, ... are mastering this journey in detail by analysing massive amounts of data and offering hyper-personalised content, attracting new customers continuously and keeping them satisfied within their loyalty loop.

3.4 Foote, Cone and Belding's matrix/grid

In previous chapters, we discussed the concept of the Customer Decision Journey and described some interesting models. Basically, it all goes back to the following standard reasoning:

step 1. a consumer has a certain "**need**" and tries to find a solution to fulfil it
step 2. a consumer evaluates the different options: both rationally (right knowledge = "**think**") and emotionally (right feelings = "**feel**")
step 3. a consumer will purchase the best solution according to them ("**do**")

But are we really following the same reasoning for each single need we might have? Do we follow the same activities in reasoning behaviour for a purchase of a car as for a purchase of a Snickers? It's obvious that this isn't the case: if we want to buy a new car, we will gather much more information than when we want to buy some kind of sweets. Depending on the type of solution, we follow a different journey.

In 1980, Richard Vaughn, Senior Vice President of the global advertising agency Foote, Cone and Belding, launched a very interesting model, which is still known as the **FCB grid**.[63] The FCB grid or the Foote, Cone and Belding matrix is an integrative approach to interpreting the consumer's buying behaviour and its implications for adopting suitable advertising strategy. With this model, they want to challenge the "Think – Feel – Do" reasoning behind all Customer Decision Journeys. It's not the only sequence for how a consumer behaves to buy a solution.

This model was designed with the help of the theory of the **right or left brain**, related to the fact that humans are using both their **emotional attributes** as well as their **rational behaviour**.

Chapter 3: Customer (Decision) Journey

The FCB Grid helps marketers classify solutions based on two dimensions: **involvement** and **thinking/feeling**.

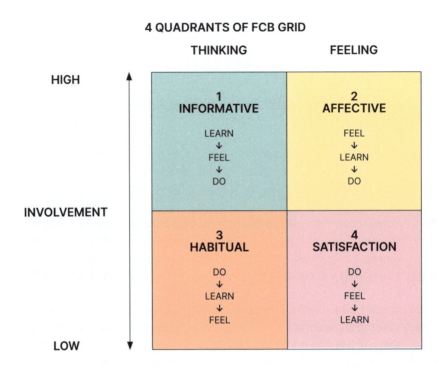

Figure 1.55: Foote, Cone & Belding grid

1. **Involvement**: This dimension refers to the **level of consumer involvement** with a certain solution. Involvement can be categorised into high involvement and low involvement.
   a. **High involvement**: Products or services that consumers are highly involved with typically require careful consideration before purchase. These types of "solutions" are not frequently bought and/or might contain a certain level of "risk" in time or money/budget.
   Examples include cars, houses, and expensive electronics or fashion.
   b. **Low involvement**: Products or services that consumers are less involved

with are usually purchased routinely or without much thought. The final decision doesn't have a huge risk itself.

Examples include everyday consumer goods like toothpaste, laundry detergent, or snacks.

2. **Thinking / Feeling**: this dimension refers to the **type of consumer response** to a solution, whether it's rational or emotional.
   a. **Thinking**: These products or services elicit a **rational** response from consumers. They are evaluated based on logical considerations such as features, benefits, and price.
   b. **Feeling**: These products or services evoke an **emotional** response from consumers. Consumers will make their decision based on how the product or service makes them feel, rather than purely rational considerations.

These 2 dimensions (each with 2 possibilities) form 4 distinctive quadrants inside the grid:
   a. "**Informative/learning**" type of products. Consumers will use more **rational** elements for their buying decisions and there's a **higher** level of involvement (as the risk of choice might be more substantial).
   b. "**Affective**" type of products. These products score also **high** in consumer involvement, though the decision is more based on feelings (**emotional**).
   c. "**Habitual/routine**" type of products. Any purchase of this type is characterised by "**low** degree of involvement" and the decision is purely based on **ratio**.
   d. "**Satisfaction/hedonistic**" products. This last group of products is purchased mainly on "feelings" (**emotional**), though the involvement degree remains **low** (as the risk will be low).

The following Figure 1.56 gives an example of the FCB grid with different product groups in each quadrant.

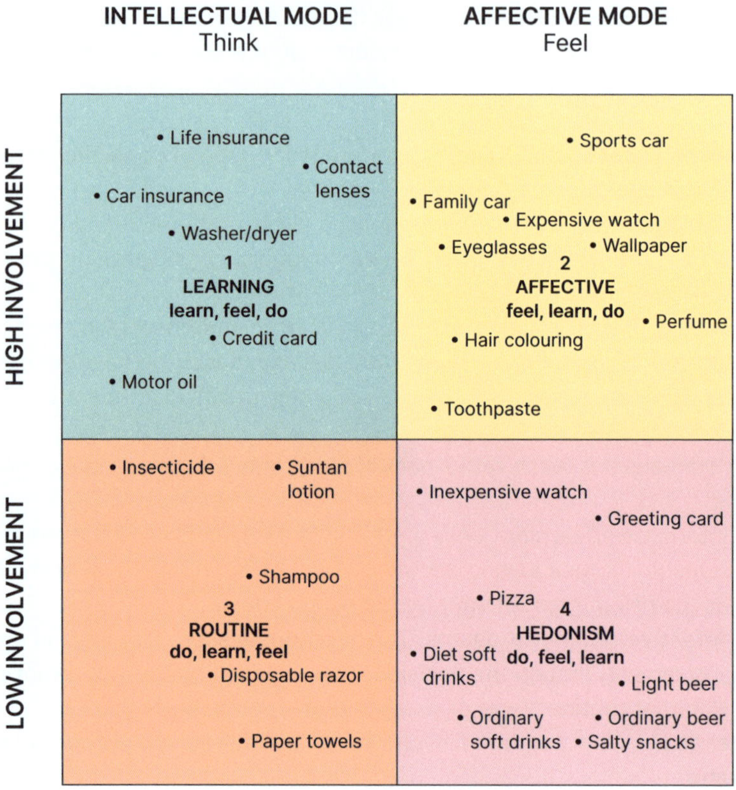

INTELLECTUAL MODE
Think

AFFECTIVE MODE
Feel

HIGH INVOLVEMENT

- Life insurance
- Contact lenses
- Car insurance
- Washer/dryer

1
LEARNING
learn, feel, do
- Credit card
- Motor oil

- Sports car
- Family car
- Expensive watch
- Eyeglasses
- Wallpaper

2
AFFECTIVE
feel, learn, do
- Perfume
- Hair colouring
- Toothpaste

LOW INVOLVEMENT

- Insecticide
- Suntan lotion
- Shampoo

3
ROUTINE
do, learn, feel
- Disposable razor
- Paper towels

- Inexpensive watch
- Greeting card
- Pizza

4
HEDONISM
do, feel, learn
- Diet soft drinks
- Light beer
- Ordinary soft drinks
- Ordinary beer
- Salty snacks

Figure 1.56: FCB grid with product groups [64]

Let's have a closer look at each quadrant.

Quadrant 1: "**Learning**" or "**Informative**" (high involvement / thinking)
Products within this quadrant follow the "**classic customer journey**". Consumers are aware of the possibilities, then they evaluate the different options, first from a rational (thinking) point of view, then from the emotional (feeling) perspective and then decide which one to choose. In general, you can describe it as follows:
1. Learning → 2. Feeling → 3. Doing.
Examples: "**insurances**", "**household appliances**", or "**energy contracts**"

110   Marketing

Quadrant 2: "**Affective**" (high involvement / feeling)

Products within the "affective" group follow almost the same reasoning as the ones from the "learning" group, but the emotional aspect will be the "trigger". Consumers will start evaluating the different options by having a good feeling (emotional) about the different options. Once convinced of their interest, they will continue to think (rational) which options might be possible (budget) and will decide on the final solution based on the answers of previous stages. Overall, the journey is as follows: **1. Feeling** → **2. Learning** → **3. Doing**.

Examples: "**cars**", "**fashion**" or "**furniture**"

Quadrant 3: "**Habitual/Routine**" (Low involvement / thinking)

As mentioned above, most of our decisions are purely "**routine**", without any effort or energy in evaluating the pros and cons of different options. This consumer behaviour is typical when searching for products of quadrant 3 (which are so-called "routine" products). If needed, we will simply buy these products based on previous purchases or maybe because of certain promotions on the shop floor (providing a sense of "making a good deal" for the consumers). Afterwards, consumers will evaluate their purchasing act by consuming these products. The evaluation of "habitual" or "routine" products will be mainly done on a rational basis. As mentioned previously, **the "risk" related to the purchasing activity is very low**, so that's why consumers decide to buy without extensive evaluations. So the consumer journey can be described as follows: **1. Doing** → **2. Learning** → **3. Feeling**.

Examples: "**toilet paper**" or "**detergents**"

Quadrant 4: "**Satisfaction/Hedonism**" (Low involvement / feeling)

Very similarly to the previous quadrant, consumers will not start intensive evaluation processes for these type of products, though they will go for the satisfactory options they've purchased before... and once consumed, this will be the basis of future purchases or not. The only difference is the fact that the evaluation is mainly done in an emotional way (feeling). The type of products we can distinguish in this quadrant are also known as our "**guilty pleasures**": we will continue to buy them, even though we understand very well that "purely rationally" these are not necessary for living. The feelings (emotions) once we have consumed these products are strong and force us to buy them...

Examples: "**sweets**", "**crisps**", or "**beer**"

Some extra information: FCB grid according to Kahneman's theory

Besides the classification, Foote, Cone and Belding found out that the "customer journey" will differ depending on the quadrant within the grid (and the product type).

The research showed them that "high involvement" purchases often take more time: consumers will not directly or instinctively decide to purchase these types of goods. They want to be both rationally and emotionally reassured about their decision, as the risk is substantial.

From Kahneman's perspective, it's more about system 2 or slow thinking and it's something we don't do all the time as it's very tiring and energy consuming (see above). Once entering the areas of "low involvement", consumers are actually more into their system 1 or fast thinking: they don't spend too much time evaluating all the existing options and will just buy the things or brands they usually do...

As mentioned by Kahneman, most of our buying decisions are led by our fast thinking system, without any form of rational nor emotional evaluation. We've bought it before ... and if we were satisfied with the result (emotional or rational), we will probably buy it again.

3.5 Some important thoughts about the "Customer Decision Journey"

The model of the "Customer Decision Journey" is widely used by so many marketers, though there are also **some points of criticism**. Here are the most important ones:
1. **Linear Assumption**: The traditional funnel metaphor, which the model builds upon, assumes a linear progression from awareness to purchase. In reality, the decision-making process is more complex and non-linear. Consumers may revisit different stages or skip steps altogether.

2. **Consumer Empowerment**: With the rise of digital channels and information availability, consumers are more empowered than ever. They actively seek out information, compare options, and engage in conversations with peers. The model doesn't fully capture this dynamic two-way communication.
3. **Business-to-Business (B2B) Context**: While the model works well for consumer markets, it may be less applicable in B2B scenarios. B2B decision journeys often involve longer and more intricate purchasing sequences, which the model doesn't fully address (more about it in one of the coming chapters).
4. **Ongoing Evolution**: Customer tastes, technology, and brand perceptions evolve over time. The model should be revisited periodically to ensure it remains relevant and aligned with changing consumer behaviour.
5. **Loyalty and Post-Purchase**: In the beginning, the believers of the model focused on the pre-purchase phases. However, post-purchase experiences and customer loyalty play a crucial role in long-term success. Ignoring these aspects could limit its effectiveness. Research proves that customer retention has a higher efficiency than focusing on getting new customers throughout the funnel leading to a higher "**Customer lifetime Value**".

Extra information: Some other "digital" models for the CDJ

Inspired by the increased speed of digitalisation, certain marketers are using different models as an alternative for the standard "Customer Decision Journey". Here are 2 examples:

1. See-Think-Do-Care model

The "**See-Think-Do-Care**" model (STDC) is a powerful framework used in marketing and communication and has been developed by Avinash Kaushik, a Google executive and marketing analytics thought leader. It encourages businesses to view their planning through the lens of the customer's perspective.[65]

SEE: This stage represents the largest addressable qualified audience (LAQA). These are individuals who are discovering your brand for the first time. Your goal here is to create awareness. Consider what it's like for a consumer to see your brand initially. What kind of experience do you want to provide? What valuable content can you offer to encourage them to think about your brand's offerings?

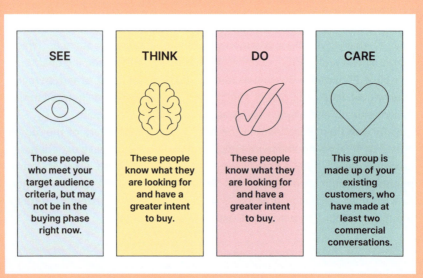

Figure 1.57: STDC – model [66]

THINK: In the Think stage, the LAQA has mild commercial intent. They are thinking about your brand's offerings. Your task is to provide content that matches their intent and interest level. Think about what will move them from considering your brand to taking action. What bridges the gap between thinking and doing?

DO: At this point, the LAQA is ready to transact. They are willing to purchase from you. When they take a "Do" action, what experience can you provide that will truly impress them? Optimise the See and Think stages to maximise the Do stage.

CARE: The Care stage involves repeat customers who have an affinity for your brand. It's about nurturing and deepening the relationship. How can you continue to engage and delight these loyal customers? Remember, caring for existing customers is just as important as acquiring new ones.

In summary, the STDC model guides marketers to tailor their content and strategies for each consideration stage, ensuring effective communication with their target audience. By understanding these intent clusters, you can build stronger relationships and drive better results.

2. RACE model

Digital companies are adept at gathering vast amounts of data to track and understand the decision journeys of their customers. From this perspective, Dr Dave Chaffey created the RACE framework in order to highlight which digital marketing activities you need to focus on to improve results from digital marketing. The RACE Framework consists of these four steps or on-line marketing activities designed to help brands engage their customers throughout the customer lifecycle: Reach → Act → Convert → Engage.

	VOLUME	QUALITY	VALUE	
REACH **Awareness** **& visits**	Unique visitors	Bounce rate	Revenue per visit	n Searches % Brand
ACT **Interaction** **& leads**	n Leads	% Conversion to lead	Goal value per visit	Page views per visit
CONVERT **Sales and** **profit**	n Sales	% Conversion to sale	Sales value	Average order value
ENGAGE **Loyalty and** **advocacy**	% Active customers	% Customer conversion	% existing sales value	n Brand mentions

Figure 1.58: RACE – model [68]

REACH. Reach involves increasing website visits and building awareness on other websites and in offline media by driving visits to different web presences like your main site, microsites or social media pages. It involves maximising reach over time to create multiple interactions using different PESO media channels.
Examples: social media platforms, search engines, display advertising, email marketing, targeted advertising, ...

ACT. Act is short for Interact. It's a separate stage since encouraging interactions on websites and in social media to generate leads is a big challenge for online marketers. It's about persuading site visitors or prospects to take the next step on their journey when they initially reach your site or social network presence. Act is also about encouraging participation. This can be sharing of content via social media or customer reviews.

Some important actions are:
· Encourage website visitors to take specific actions, such as signing up for newsletters, downloading resources, or engaging with content.
· Optimise website design and user experience.
· Implement calls-to-action (CTA) to prompt users to take the next step in their journey.

CONVERT. This is conversion to "sale" or going for the final deal – either online or offline. Focus on turning engaged users into (paying) customers. Implement strategies such as targeted promotions, personalised recommendations, and retargeting campaigns to incentivise conversions.

ENGAGE. This is engagement that develops a long-term relationship with first-time buyers to build customer loyalty as repeat purchases, by using customer communications on your site, social presence, email and direct interactions to boost customer lifetime value.
Utilise email marketing, social media engagement, and customer feedback mechanisms to maintain regular interaction with customers.

This RACE model is also known in digital marketing as the strategy of "lead generation", seen as a strategic process aimed at attracting and capturing potential customers (or leads) who have shown interest in a company's products or services. The primary goal of lead generation is to initiate and cultivate relationships with these prospects, converting them into (paying) customers and ultimately keeping this relationship close for a longer term optimising the Customer Lifetime Value.

3.6 Overview on "Customer Decision Journey"

a. The concept of the Customer Decision Journey ("CDJ") is the process that a consumer goes through from initial awareness of a product or service (solution) over the decision to make the purchase/deal to the final experience activities.
b. Since the beginning, there have been several models that explain this type of consumer behaviour:
   - AIDA
   - McKinsey
   - Flip the Funnel
c. The "customer decision journey" might be different related to the type of "solution". The FCB grid helped to distinguish these differences of behaviour, by splitting up the products and services into 4 quadrants based on 2 dimensions:
   - High vs low involvement
   - "Thinking" (rational) vs "Feeling" (emotional)

Chapter 4:
SAVE & CDJ... the "perfect" marriage

We've tackled 2 key models for marketeers: the SAVE model helps us to define the actions to frame your marketing plan and the Customer Decision Journey explains the results of your marketing activities on desired consumer behaviour. But how can both models come together:
- Should we start with Solution or Access or Education?
- In which stages should we focus on Solution, Access, or Education?
- And what about Value?

In other words, where do we implement the different SAVE parts related to the different CDJ phases and what is the reason that this would lead to the "perfect" marketing marriage?

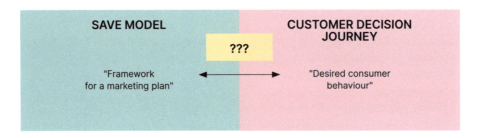

Figure 1.59: The marriage of SAVE and CDJ

4.1 General recommendations

As mentioned above, the **customer decision journey** can be described as a serial, multiple-step approach, all linked to each other. Depending on different factors like knowledge, emotions, or other personal elements, customers will proceed slower or faster throughout this process. Within each step, this "linearity" will be less relevant and will be more difficult to manage as a marketer.

In the coming paragraphs, we're going to describe how to optimise each phase by focusing on the right SAVE – tools.

4.1.1 First phase: "awareness" through "Solution" & "Education"

To start any kind of journey, potential customers need a certain **trigger** to proceed. Mostly, they will experience a **certain type of** "**awareness**" **of an existing or latent need**. This might be both consciously or unconsciously. Without any form of consideration, customers will not start spending time or energy in evaluating possible provided opportunities.

This "need" can easily be triggered by focusing on the "Solution" part of your marketing strategy. As described above, all efforts that marketers put into practice to explain possible "problems" or "challenges" and the way to solve them all aim to create "awareness" for a certain need amongst prospective customers.

Besides the "Solution" activities, which target the "needs" more, it's important to combine these with the correct "Education" strategies. In particular, we are referring to the 3H model, where the HERO content is the optimal choice to grow "awareness" around your "Solution".

Example: Apple Vision Pro (Phase 1)

Figure 1.60: Apple Vision Pro [69/70]

When Apple launched their headset Vision Pro, they did it by explaining and demonstrating all the possible features with their newest innovation. They made up movies, articles, and other press material to express their "Solution" to the public.

Chapter 4: SAVE & CDJ... the "perfect" marriage

Besides these standard elements of "HERO" content, they probably invited all kinds of influencers and journalists to try out the Vision Pro in real life so they could experience it themselves, leading to massive content on different (social) media channels ("Education"). By executing it in this way, Apple created a big bang on the market creating "awareness" amongst technology-savvy people, ready to start their own customer decision journey.

Example 2: Feeling "hungry"

Figure 1.61: Feeling "hungry" [71]

Sometimes people are "unconsciously" starting this journey even when there's no specific communication that might trigger them. Let's consider that you sense a certain uncomfortable feeling in your stomach at lunch time. It's clear that you are getting hungry (= "awareness" of a need) and you're looking for possible options (= "Solution") that might overcome this need. Based on common knowledge and personal preferences (= "Education"), you will start your journey and you will search for the food possibilities in the neighbourhood.

Summary:
Igniting the customer decision journey (= **PHASE 1**) means triggering awareness in prospective customers of their needs. This can be done by focusing on activities around "**Solution**" and "**Education**", and, in particular, **HERO content**.

4.1.2 Second phase: "active evaluation" through "Access" and "Education"

Convinced about their need, a consumer will **look for all the necessary information to make a choice** amongst the portfolio of "Solutions" and to fulfil it. They will **start searching** on different channels both offline and online, making sure **the risk of making a bad choice is minimised**. This is exactly where marketers want to help them with the "Access" strategy (see above). This element focuses on making sure that all the information about their Solution is available to potential customers and how they can get it ("deal").

Again, the "Access" strategy won't do the job by itself. It needs to go hand in hand with the other elements of "Education". In the first place, it's important to link this part with the HYGIENE or HELP elements from the 3H model, as it is the type of content customers are deliberately searching for (to fulfil their need). Depending on the type of "Solution", this stage might be reassuring enough for the prospective customer to go to the next phase (no clear risks), though sometimes they still have some doubts and need some more information. In the latter situation, marketers will tap into the other part of the "Education" strategy and focus on providing HUB content to their prospects. These frequently posted and "engaging" pieces of information aim to improve the relationship between prospects and proposed "Solutions" in order to keep the "awareness" level alive and minimise the risk that eventually will lead the prospects to proceed to the next phase. Remember that perfect HUB content might be all kinds of guarantees to after-sales services. This will reassure the prospective customer so that they finalise the deal, especially after having evaluated all the options carefully.

Example: Apple Vision Pro (Phase 2)

Figure 1.62: Apple Vision Pro: product page [72]

Let's get back to the Apple Vision Pro example from the previous chapter. A prospective customer might be interested in this innovation and will start to look at all the possible elements needed to make a decision to buy it (or not). Firstly, they will look for information like features, price, and possibilities to buy (= "HYGIENE" or "HELP" content). You can define these under the "Access" strategy. As it's something brand new and considering the budget, it's clear that this customer will also evaluate this Vision Pro Solution with other Solutions, offered by other brands.

On the other hand, several reviews and posted messages from influencers seem to be very positive. Moreover the same customer might have a good relationship with Apple, thanks to previous purchase brand experiences with that brand. In the end, the Apple after-sales service is always available if there are any questions or issues with using the devices. All the "HUB" content might help the customer in their journey to decide on the Apple solution, which will lead them to proceed to the next step.

Example: Phase 2 according to FCB model

Figure 1.63: FCB [73]

Most of the time, consumers don't consciously evaluate all the possible options to go the next step of getting the deal. They might skip most of the actions as they will proceed almost directly to the next step based on the existing HYGIENE content they find. This is mainly the case when dealing with "needs" with very limited risks in the decision choice.

Examples can be found under the "Routine" (e.g. detergents) and "Satisfaction/Hedonism" (e.g. sweets) categories of the Foote, Cone and Belding model (see above). Being "top of mind" amongst customers will be the main objective for these kind of brands.

Some extra information: The evaluation according to Kahneman

Once a potential customer is "aware" of the existence of a possible need, they might consider continuing their journey by doing all the actions needed to evaluate all possible options that fulfil this need.

This might be done both unconsciously (= system 2 thinking (Kahneman)) and consciously (= system 1 thinking (Kahneman)).

Summary:
Being aware of an existing "need" will start the "active evaluation" of all possible Solutions that might exist to fulfil it (= **PHASE 2**). Prospects will start to look for the information needed to make the right decision and minimise all possible risks. This is fully covered by the "**Access**" and "**Education**" strategies. In the first place, it might be interesting to focus on the **HYGIENE** or **HELP** content, as this is the type of information these types of customers will search for. If this content is not convincing enough, you can continue with the **HUB** content, which is frequent and engaging information that tries to overcome existing doubts and to reassure the customer to take the next step in its customer decision journey: going for the deal.

4.1.3 Third phase: "closing the deal" through "Access" and "Value"

The prospect has finally made up their mind: after (carefully) evaluating all possible options, they will choose the "Solution" that optimally fulfils their need. This means:
  a. The Solution is clear and in line with the existing need.
  b. The Access strategy is convincing enough to overcome possible risks.
  c. The Education strategy helps to influence the customer in their decision.

In the end, you can sum it up by saying: the Solutions offer the best "**Value**". As described above, the Value component is made up of the other 3 elements from the SAVE model. At the same time, it's important as marketer to optimise your "**Access**" possibilities, making sure that the prospect can easily close the deal. It would be a pity to lose a convinced potential customer who doesn't know how to close the deal.

Example: Apple Vision Pro (Phase 3)

Figure 1.64: Apple (Online) Store [74] / [75]

Back to the Apple Vision Pro case. It's very probable that prospects will evaluate this purchase very carefully. They will look at several articles and websites to get a good view on the pros and cons of it.

In the end, they will even try it out in one of the special Apple stores to see if it's really worthwhile paying the considerable amount of several thousands of euros (maybe by comparing it with other glasses from competitors). Once convinced about the total Value of this Apple tool, they will need to find the best way to buy it (offline or online), knowing that the purchase will probably ask for online registration to guarantee optimal use of the after-sales tool.

Example: A bottle of water

Figure 1.65: a bottle of water as a "value" element [76]

Chapter 4: SAVE & CDJ... the "perfect" marriage   125

When buying Solutions that have more "limited" risks (for example when you're "feeling thirsty"), it's clear that this need might be fulfilled quicker than in the case of the previous example above (Apple Vision Pro). Of course, it all depends which situation you're sitting in: in the middle of a city or under the burning sun in the desert. In both cases, a bottle of water might be a possible "Solution", though the "Access" possibilities will be different, which will impact its "Value": this will be much higher in the latter moment.

Summary:
Closing the deal (= **PHASE 3**) will only be possible if the **Value** of the proposed Solution is at its optimal level. This **optimal Value position** is made up by the **best possible combination** of the other 3 components:
- **a. Best Solution**
- **b. Best Access** (both from information and from purchasing perspective)
- **c. Best Education**

Once the prospect has acquired the Solution, they can be seen as a "real" customer, ready to use it in order to fulfil the existing need and to proceed to the final phase of the Customer Decision Journey.

4.1.4 Final phase: "Post purchase evaluation" through "Value", "Access", "Education", & "Solution"

The customer has finally chosen a certain Solution and will start "consuming" it. They will start the last stage of the process of this journey... and maybe the most important one for all parties.

Entering the last step of the journey, the customer will use the Solution and will **evaluate** it: **is everything in line with the pre-purchase expectations and can the Value be met?** This is an important element for the future relationship the customer will continue to have with the company behind the Solution (see the "trigger" star in McKinsey's Customer Decision Journey model above):
- a. A "**positive**" post-purchase evaluation (= the final Value of the Solution after

purchase and consumption remains the same or even increases) can stimulate the customer to spread this positive news to others, which can initiate new journeys amongst new potential customers.

b. A **"negative"** post-purchase evaluation (= the Value of the Solution after consumption decreases as the Solution itself disappoints) can also initiate "negative" word of mouth which can discourage new customers to choose this Solution.

Brilliant marketers will try to keep an eye on this "post-purchase" evaluation, as this customer might influence his peers about their experiences both positively or negatively. You can consider this as an equal part of the Education strategy, developed at the first phases of the journey (see previous paragraphs). This is why a customer-centric "Access" strategy is crucial to hold a close relationship with your existing customers. Most of the time, this is the objective of well-conceived HUB content (like newsletters, events, …) keeping track of the relationship with their customers. In the end, this strategy can also help to trigger the awareness of new or extra needs that can lead to new offered Solutions. This way, the customer gets into the so-called "loyalty loop" and the customer decision journey starts again. This reasoning is visually very clear in McKinsey's Customer Decision Journey model.

Example: Post-purchase evaluation

Figure 1.66: High vs low involvement brands [77]

The post-purchase evaluation is the most powerful phase in the customer decision journey process and is the same for high Value solutions (like the

Chapter 4: SAVE & CDJ... the "perfect" marriage

Apple Vision Pro) as well as very "routine" or "hedonistic/satisfaction" type of products (like toilet paper or ice cream). The customer will consume the purchased Solution and will evaluate it positively or negatively. This was also mentioned in Foote, Cone and Belding's model. The higher valued solutions may have bigger consequences, as the purchase itself took more time and energy because the customer considered it more "risky" than standard deals.

At the same time, marketers of both types of Solutions will try to retain awareness amongst their customers and will try to establish a long-term relationship, by stimulating repurchases or looking for opportunities (= new "needs") for them.

As you might notice, "Value" indirectly plays a role in all the steps of the customer decision journey, as it increases gradually from phase 1 to phase 2 by growing through knowledge and emotional feeling to finalising the deal in phase 3 and keeping promises in phase 4 (or not).

Summary:
At the end of the customer decision journey, all elements of the SAVE model play an important role in establishing a long-term relationship (and re-igniting the "loyalty loop"):
a. The **Value** after the post-purchase evaluation needs to at least remain the same or may increase.
b. This will have certain consequences on the **Education** strategy towards peers and others (reviews, user-generated content, ...).
c. Keeping a close relationship with existing customers can help to spread positive messages and to keep an eye on post-purchase activities (which is part of the **Access** strategy and more particularly the **HUB** content).
d. Thanks to this relationship, marketers can initiate new journeys towards other **Solutions** by instigating new "needs" amongst customers.

4.1.5 Overview

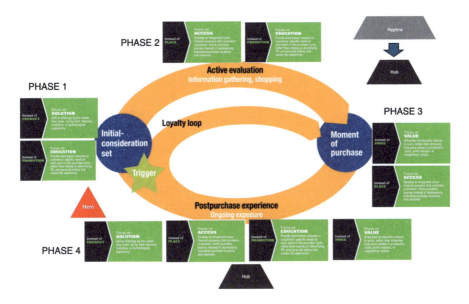

Figure 1.67: combination of models: SAVE, Customer Decision Journey & 3H

4.2 Measuring Value: focus on "trust" factor

In the end, marketing can be considered as **the science of optimising value for your customers**. This value component increases all through the journey from awareness to consideration and interest to conversion and remains high in the post-purchase moments.

It's clear that this "Value" is closely correlated with the parameter of **TRUST** that a person or company might have in the proposed solution (brand, product, or service). **A high level of trust from customers in the solution means that they see limited risks in a (possible) relationship and they assign a high value to it.** This level of "trust" shows the same trend over the Customer Decision Journey: minimal in the beginning, growing in the second phase, coming to a local "top" level when deciding for the deal and hopefully continuing to grow after the conversion phase.

To measure this level of "trust" all over the journey, it's important to carry out some research with some specific questions.

a. **Key questions in the "first" phase of the journey**
In the beginning, it's all about measuring the level of "awareness": are you aware of the existence of a particular "Solution" (product, brand, or service)? We can distinguish 2 different types of "awareness": **recognition** and **recall**. When customers are prompted by a particular name, they have aided awareness, also called recognition. Unaided awareness, also known as recall, occurs when people can recall a solution without any form of encouragement (name, logo, jingle/sound, …). It's clear that recall is much stronger than recognition. "Top of mind" awareness/recall is the first name/brand that pops up on the list of recall names.

It's clear that brands that are stuck in this phase, have **a very limited level of trust**.

Figure 1.68: Levels of awareness [78]

b. Key questions in the "second" (evaluation) phase

Once you're a more "known" solution, it's important to research how this one is perceived by possible prospects. It's all about asking potential customers about the elements of the "brand identity" of the solution (see "brand models" of Kapferer and Keller above). Some interesting ones are:

1. **Image:** This refers to the **overall perception or impression** that consumers have about a particular solution. It encompasses various aspects such as the reputation, visual identity (like logos, colours, and typography), messaging, and the emotional connections consumers associate with the solution.
2. **Attitude:** This reflects consumers' **overall evaluations, feelings, and beliefs** about a solution. Positive attitudes typically lead to favourable behaviours such as purchase intent, loyalty, and advocacy, while negative attitudes can result in avoidance or disengagement.
3. **Personality:** This is a set of human characteristics or traits attributed to a particular solution. Brands often try to embody specific personality traits to appeal to their target audience and differentiate themselves in the market. These personality traits can include attributes like sincerity, excitement, competence, sophistication, etc. Personality helps consumers **relate to and connect with the brand** on a more emotional level.

Qualitative and quantitative surveys will measure on which level a certain solution is situated. **The more "positive" responses on image, attitude and/or personality, the higher the level of trust**. As mentioned above, it's the objective of a clear content plan (especially Hygiene & HUB) to improve these aspects.

c. Key questions in the "conversion" phase

Marketers will also look at how "trustful" their solution is on the "purchase intention" side. Typical questions such as "How likely would you buy/choose/use solution X?" are used to qualify the intention of prospects on the conversion level. **Highly trusted solutions will encounter less issues as these customers attribute high value to them**.

d. Key questions in the "post-purchase" phase

Ultimately, it's clear that the trust remains high (enough) so that the relationship between a customer and its solution remains close.

A metric to measure customer loyalty and satisfaction (and trust) is the **Net Promoter Score (NPS)**, introduced by Fred Reichheld in 2003. NPS is widely used across various industries as a simple yet powerful tool to assess customer sentiment.

How it works:
Customers are typically asked a single question: **"On a scale of 0 to 10, how likely are you to recommend our product/service to a friend or colleague?"** Based on their response, customers are categorised into three groups:
1. Promoters (score 9-10): These are highly satisfied customers who are likely to recommend the product or service to others.
2. Passives (score 7-8): These customers are satisfied but not enthusiastic. They are less likely to actively promote your product or service.
3. Detractors (score 0-6): These customers are dissatisfied and may even spread negative feedback about your product or service.

The NPS is calculated by subtracting the percentage of Detractors from the percentage of Promoters. Passives are not included in the calculation. The resulting score can range from -100 to +100. Having a positive score means that your solution has more promoters than detractors, so most of your customers are satisfied and will likely recommend you. The negative score means the opposite and reflects a less positive situation.

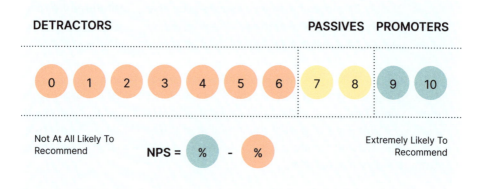

Figure 1.69: Net Promoter Score [79]

NPS not only provides a numerical value but also helps in identifying areas for improvement. Companies can analyse feedback from promoters and detractors to understand what they are doing well and what needs to be improved. Promoters can be encouraged to advocate for the brand, while detractors can be engaged to address their concerns and potentially turn them into promoters.

Very important remark:
As the NPS calculation is very "category" driven (certain markets are more customer focused than others), you need to evaluate these scores within the same category.

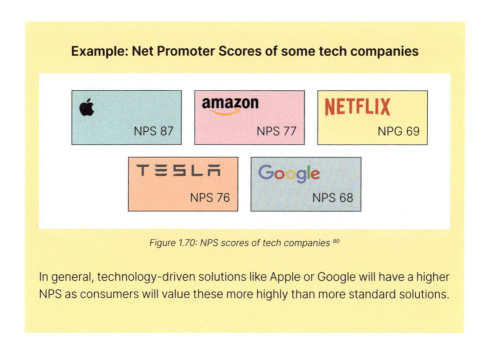

Figure 1.70: NPS scores of tech companies [80]

In general, technology-driven solutions like Apple or Google will have a higher NPS as consumers will value these more highly than more standard solutions.

It's important to conduct these different types of surveys repeatedly over time, so you can distinguish a certain evolution in "trust" around your solution. Doing it only once will be a waste of time and money.

Chapter 5:
Some general remarks

In the previous chapters, we've basically focused on 2 main concepts of marketing:
   a. SAVE model
   b. Customer Decision Journey

And how both can be merged in order to optimise your strategy to reach (potential) customers.

In the next sections, we would like to describe 2 major existing trends and their impact on the marketing concepts we've described so far:
   a. The digitalisation revolution of Artificial Intelligence (AI)
   b. The growing economies in B2B business

5.1 The era of artificial intelligence

Artificial Intelligence (AI) refers to the simulation of human intelligence in machines that are programmed to think, learn, and problem solve like humans. AI systems can perform tasks that typically require human intelligence, such as recognising speech, making decisions, understanding natural language, and interpreting visual data.

It will transform the modern marketing landscape in various ways. Here's a general overview of how AI can influence marketing practices:
1. **Personalisation**
   - **Customer Segmentation**: AI can analyse vast amounts of data to identify distinct consumer segments based on behaviour, preferences, and demographics. This allows for highly targeted marketing campaigns.
   - **Customised Content**: AI-driven tools can create personalised content and recommendations for individual users, enhancing consumer engagement and conversion rates.
2. **Predictive Analytics**
   - **Demand Forecasting**: AI can predict future trends and consumer demands

by analysing historical data and market patterns. This helps businesses optimise inventory and marketing strategies.

- **Customer Behaviour**: Predictive analytics can anticipate consumer actions, such as the likelihood of purchase, enabling proactive measures to retain customers and increase sales.

3. Automation

- **Chatbots and Virtual Assistants**: AI-powered chatbots can handle customer inquiries and provide instant support, improving customer satisfaction and freeing up human resources for more complex tasks.
- **Automated Campaigns**: AI can automate marketing tasks such as email campaigns, social media posting, and ad placement, ensuring timely and efficient execution.

4. Data Analysis

- **Sentiment Analysis**: AI can analyse social media posts, reviews, and feedback to gauge public sentiment towards a brand or product. This helps marketers understand customer opinions and adjust strategies accordingly.
- **A/B Testing**: AI can conduct and analyse A/B tests more efficiently, determining the most effective marketing strategies and tactics.

5. Content Creation

- **Automated Writing**: AI tools can generate written content, such as product descriptions, blog posts, and social media updates, saving time and maintaining consistency.
- **Visual and Video Content**: AI can assist in creating and editing visual content, including images and videos, enhancing the quality and appeal of marketing materials.

6. Customer Experience

- **Enhanced Customer Interactions**: AI can provide a more seamless and engaging customer experience through personalised recommendations, predictive customer support, and interactive interfaces.
- **Loyalty Programmes**: AI can optimise loyalty programmes by analysing customer data to offer personalised rewards and incentives that increase customer retention.

7. Advertising

- **Programmatic Advertising**: AI can automate the buying of digital advertising space, targeting the right audience at the right time with the right message, thus improving the efficiency and effectiveness of ad spend.

Impact on previous models:
- **Solution**: sharper segmentations, possibility of microtargeting, personalised campaigns
- **Access**: smooth and easy flow within the Customer Decision Journey, 24/7 service with a personalised approach focused on your specific "need" or issue
- **Education**: tailored content based on data, more efficient and effective campaigns, increased level of loyalty, ...
- **Value**: All the elements above should lead to a higher level of Value (and "trust") as long as the customer is open to sharing their data with these AI tools.

This list of AI-powered tools has been AI-generated and is far from exhaustive. It's clear that the standard marketing models and techniques will still continue to be relevant, though **the use of AI will help marketeers to optimise their use efficiently and effectively**.

5.2 B2C vs B2B: same challenges... different settings...

B2B and B2C are two acronyms that get thrown around regularly:
- **B2B** stands for **business-to-business**, referring to a type of transaction that takes place between one business and another.
- **B2C** stands for **business-to-consumer**, as in a transaction that takes place between a business and an individual as the end customer.

Both types of businesses follow the same techniques and models in marketing, though there are some important differences between them. These differences are mainly situated in the following areas:
- a. Target audience
- b. Decision-making process (sales cycle)
- c. Marketing strategies: content and channels

B2B	VS	B2C
Lower volume, higher price		Higher volume, lower price
Education, efficiency		Entertainment, convenience
Interpersonal relationships		Transactional relationships
Logic and features		Desires and benefits
Long-term goals		Short-term goals
Long sales cycle		Short sales cycle

Figure 1.71: B2B vs B2C [81]

5.2.1 B2B

B2B marketing targets other businesses, organisations, or professionals. These audiences are typically decision-makers within companies, such as executives, managers, or procurement officers.

The **decision-making process** in B2B marketing is **often longer and involves multiple stakeholders**. Purchases are **usually high-value** and require **extensive** research, evaluation, and approval from several departments. Decisions are primarily driven by logic, **ROI (Return on Investment), efficiency, and long-term value**. Businesses look for products or services that will improve their operations or profitability.

We can primarily distinguish the following marketing strategies:
- **Content Marketing:** Producing detailed, informative content such as white papers, case studies, eBooks, and webinars to educate and inform potential clients.
- **Personalised Outreach:** Tailored communications and relationship-building activities, including direct emails, personalised presentations, and one-on-

one meetings.
- **Trade Shows and Conferences**: Participating in industry-specific events to network and showcase products/services directly to potential business clients.

The channels, used for establishing first contact with potential customers (leads), are social media (like LinkedIn, but also the consumer-based ones, like Facebook or YouTube), email marketing and very specialised industry publications (like niche industry magazines, ...) and websites.

5.2.2 B2C

B2C marketing targets individual consumers who are the end-users of products or services. The audience is broad and diverse, encompassing different demographics and psychographics.

The **decision-making process** is usually **quicker**, as consumers often make purchase decisions **impulsively** or based on **personal preferences**. Decisions are driven by **emotional triggers, personal desires, brand perception, and social influences**. Factors like convenience, price, and aesthetic appeal play significant roles.

The main marketing strategies used by marketers of B2C companies are:
- **Mass Marketing**: Using broad-reaching campaigns to create brand awareness and attract a large audience.
- **Promotions and Discounts**: Offering time-limited discounts, coupons, and special offers to drive quick purchases.
- **Engaging Content**: Creating entertaining and visually appealing content that resonates with consumers' lifestyles and interests, such as videos, blog posts, and social media updates.

So the general and broad communication and distribution channels are largely frequented by B2C marketers in search of potential consumers:
a. Social Media Platforms
b. Retail and eCommerce
c. All kinds of digital and traditional media, ...

Part 2:
Strategic marketing

Chapter 1:
General introduction to strategic marketing

In part 1, we tackled the main models and theories that are necessary to exploit your marketing opportunities in short-term actions. It all comes down to driving certain actions that are related to 2 main models: the SAVE model on one hand, and the Customer Decision Journey on the other.

Of course, as a marketer you can't just rely on the execution of these 2 models. Before diving into the tactical complexities of the operational marketing plan, it is paramount to lay a solid foundation through **strategic marketing**.

Strategic marketing involves the high-level planning and decision-making that shapes the overarching **direction** of an organisation's marketing efforts. It encompasses a comprehensive analysis of market conditions, competitive landscape, consumer behaviour, and internal capabilities. This stage is about setting **long-term goals**, defining a unique value proposition, and identifying target segments that align with the organisation's strengths and market opportunities. This is a process that ensures all subsequent marketing activities are coherent, aligned, and focused on **achieving sustainable competitive advantage**.

In the coming sections we will guide you through the following structure that frames this strategic process:

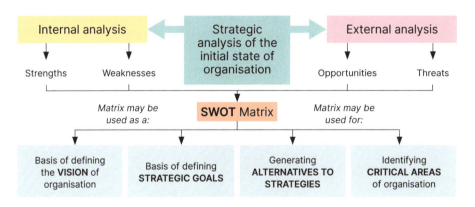

Figure 2.1: Strategic marketing process [82]

As presented in the chart above, the process will proceed through several steps:
a. Step 1: Strategic overview
b. Step 2: External analysis (which will lead to "Opportunities" and "Threats")
c. Step 3: Internal analysis (which will lead to "Strengths" and "Weaknesses")
d. Step 4: SWOT matrix
e. Step 5: Going from strategy to operational marketing (Strategic options)

This process is mostly evaluated on a yearly base to make sure that the strategic goals are still applicable. It all depends on the market you're operating in. We will describe each step in the following sections.

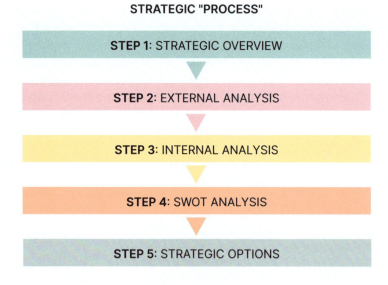

Figure 2.2: The different steps in strategic analysis

Chapter 2:
Strategic process

Let's dive deeper into this process…

2.1 Step 1: Strategic overview

Before starting the strategic process, you need to describe the **starting situation of your company**. It all comes back to the main question: **Who are you exactly and what's your reason for being in the market?** It consists of certain key elements, which create the strategic guidelines for your company and which need to be seen as one "organic" entity:
   a. Mission statement
   b. Vision statement
   c. Strategic goals
   d. Company Values

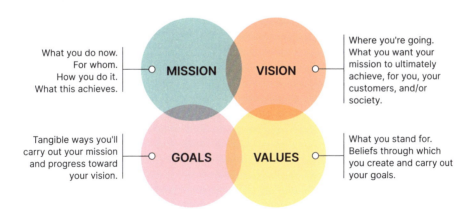

Figure 2.3: Strategic guidelines of an organisation [83]

2.1.1 Mission statement

A **mission** statement is a brief description of the overarching meaning of the company or nonprofit. It attempts to succinctly explain **why a company exists and what its purpose is**. Brilliant mission will also capture the target audience of the organisation (stakeholders, employees, customers, ...).

Overall, a mission statement serves as a guiding light for the company's strategic planning, decision-making, and daily operations, ensuring that all efforts are aligned with its core purpose and long-term vision.

Example: Mission statement of Swarovski

Figure 2.4: Swarovski jewellery [84]

This is the mission statement of Swarovski:

> Swarovski adds sparkle to everyday life with high-quality products and services that exceed our customers' desires. We inspire our colleagues with innovation and reward their achievements while striving to expand our market leadership.

2.1.2 Vision statement

A **vision** statement describes what a company desires to achieve in the long run, generally in a timeframe of five to ten years, or sometimes even longer. It depicts a vision of what the company will look like in the future and sets a defined direction for the planning and execution of corporate-level strategies. It gives an answer to **where the organisation wants to go**. It's obvious that a vision always encapsulates a certain "**future**" element in its statement.

Example: Vision statement of Tesla

Figure 2.5: Tesla [85]

This is the vision statement of Tesla:

To create the most compelling car company of the 21st century by driving the world's transition to electric vehicles.

2.1.3 (Strategic) goals

Strategic goals are **specific, long-term objectives** that a company sets for itself to achieve its desired future state, and refers to the precise targets and outcomes that it endeavours to attain within a defined timeframe – generally the next three to five years. These strategic goals are both financial and non-financial, so they can take a lot of different forms depending on the organisation's particular business model.

In a way, those strategic goals are a bridge between the company's overall vision and its day-to-day operations. By defining clear and achievable goals, a company can ensure that all stakeholders are working towards the same end and that resources are being used effectively to achieve its business goals. In a nutshell, strategic goals are telling their target audience **how they will achieve their vision**.

> ### Examples: Strategic goals
>
> Strategic goals might include the following items:
> - Market position: growing the share of current and new markets
> - Innovation: creating new products and services, developing new skills and expertise
> - Productivity: producing more with less of any given input (financial capital, time, energy, for example)
> - Profitability: generating stronger financial results
> - Human resources: selecting and developing qualified employees
>
> Social, environmental, or development impact: products, services, or business activities that create jobs, improve societal well-being or conserve or preserve natural resources.

It's clear that these objectives target a large group of stakeholders... far more than only customers or consumers. A company needs to keep a good relationship with financial institutions and shareholders, employees, and (world) communities.

2.1.4 Values

The **values** of a company are the **fundamental beliefs and guiding principles** that shape its culture, influence its behaviour, and define its identity. These values serve as a **moral compass** for the organisation and are integral to its decision-making processes, interactions with stakeholders, and overall operations.

Example: Values of IKEA

Figure 2.6: IKEA [86]

The values of IKEA are:
- Togetherness
- Caring for people and the planet
- Cost-consciousness
- Simplicity
- Renew and improve
- Different with a meaning
- Give and take responsibility
- Lead by example

Most of the time, these values are important criteria in the process of recruitment of people. HR people will assess candidates to predict if they "embody" the same values.

2.2 Step 2: External analysis

In the philosophy of strategic planning, a company's mission, vision, and core values lay the foundational framework that defines its purpose, aspirations, and ethical compass serving as guiding lights, shaping the company's long-term objectives, and driving internal cohesion.

To effectively chart a path toward these goals, it is crucial to complement this internal clarity with a thorough **external analysis**. This involves systematically examining the **competitive landscape, market forces, customer preferences, and broader economic trends**.

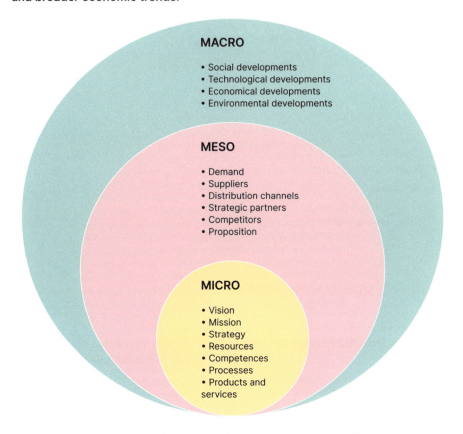

Figure 2.7: Different types of organisational environments [87]

In general there are 3 environments that are interesting for an organisation:
a. **Micro**: the internal drivers within that organisation (see next section "Internal analysis")
b. **Meso**: the "direct" external forces (customers, suppliers, competition)
c. **Macro**: the overall external "trends"

The **external analysis** focuses on the 2 latter environments (Meso and Macro). By researching the Meso- and Macro-situation, you will find information (data) that will be categorised as "Opportunities" or "Threats":

- "**Opportunities**" are elements from Meso / Macro that might help the company to **grow** (**positive** effect)
- "**Threats**" are elements from Meso / Macro that might push the company to **losses** (**negative** effect)

There are certain models that will help us to analyse these areas:
- Models to analyse the **Meso** environment:
- Five Forces Model by Porter
- Strategic models of Porter / Treacy and Wiersema
- Strategy matrices (BCG / GE)
- Model to analyse **Macro** environment:
- DESTEP (or PESTLE)

It's preferable to start your **external analysis** with the Meso environment, as this area is closer to the company (Micro) and will procure accurate information about the market situation.

2.2.1 External analysis: Meso environment

In the coming sections, we will describe the different models that will be used to analyse the Meso environment.

MODELS TO ANALYSE THE "MESO" ENVIRONMENT

a. **5 forces model of Porter**
b. **Strategy models:**
  · porter
  · Treacy & Wiersema
c. **strategic matrices:**
  · Boston Consulting Group (BCG)
  · General Electric (GE)

Figure 2.8: Different models to analyse the MESO environment (External analysis)

2.2.1.1 Five Forces Model (Porter)

The first tool to start your "external" analysis is the model elaborated by Michael Porter in the late '70s: the **"Five Forces Model"**.[88] This framework analyses the level of competition within an industry and develops business strategies. The model identifies five forces that determine the competitive intensity and attractiveness of a market:

a. Rivalry among existing competition
b. Threat of new entrants
c. Threat of substitute solutions
d. Bargaining power of suppliers
e. Bargaining power of Buyers (customers)

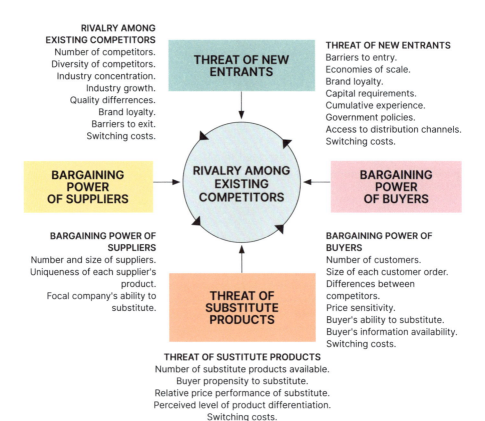

Figure 2.9: Porter's 5 forces model

This model helps you to look at each of the "individual" forces through different factors, in order to evaluate the existing "threat" as "high" (and "more negative" for the company) or "low" (and "more positive" for the company).

a. **Rivalry among existing competition**
   This force examines the **intensity of competition** among existing firms in the industry.
   Some factors that might influence this force:
   - **Number of Competitors**: More competitors increase rivalry.
   - **Size of Competitors**: Bigger competitors might have more means to invest in marketing, ...
   - **Industry Growth**: Slow growth leads to increased rivalry for market share.
   - **Fixed Costs**: High fixed costs encourage firms to fill capacity, often leading to price wars.
   - **Product Differentiation**: Low differences between competing companies increase rivalry as firms compete on price.

   Intense rivalry reduces profitability as firms engage in competitive actions like price cutting and increased marketing.

b. **Threat of new entrants**
   This force examines **how easy or difficult** it is for new competitors to enter the industry.
   Some factors that might influence this force:
   - **Barriers to Entry**: High capital requirements, strong brand identity, access to distribution channels, government regulations, economies of scale, and customer loyalty.
   - **Expected Retaliation**: The potential response from existing competitors to new entrants.

   If entry barriers are low, the threat of new entrants is high, increasing competition.

c. **Threat of substitute solutions**
   Substitutes are solutions that can fulfil the **same need or function** as the ones produced by a given industry, but come from **a different industry**.

Chapter 2: Strategic process   153

> ### Example: Substitute solutions
>
> - Tea as a substitute for coffee
> - Electric scooters as a substitute for public transport or cars

This force considers the **availability** of alternative solutions that can replace the industry's offerings.

Some factors that might influence this force:
- **Relative Price and Performance**: If a substitute offers better value, the threat is higher.
- **Switching Costs**: Low switching costs increase the threat of substitutes.

The same rules as the ones coming from direct competition are applicable: high threat of substitutes can limit price levels and reduce profitability.

d. Bargaining power of suppliers

This force looks at the **power** that **suppliers** have over firms in the industry.

Some factors that might influence this force:
- **Number of Suppliers**: Few suppliers mean higher power.
- **Uniqueness of Supplier's Product**: If suppliers offer a unique or highly differentiated solution, their power increases.
- **Switching Costs**: High costs for switching suppliers increase supplier power.

Strong supplier power can increase input costs and reduce profitability.

e. Bargaining power of Buyers (customers)

This force assesses the **power** that **customers** have over businesses.

Some factors that might influence this force:
- **Number of Buyers**: Few large buyers have more power.
- **Product Differentiation**: If solutions are standardised, buyers have more choices and thus more power.

- **Price Sensitivity**: High price sensitivity increases buyer power.
- **Switching Costs**: Low switching costs for buyers increase their power.

High buyer power can force prices down and demand higher quality or more services.

By analysing these five forces, companies can understand the competitive dynamics of their industry and develop strategies to enhance their competitive position, such as finding ways to raise barriers to entry, improving product differentiation, or establishing stronger relationships with suppliers and buyers.

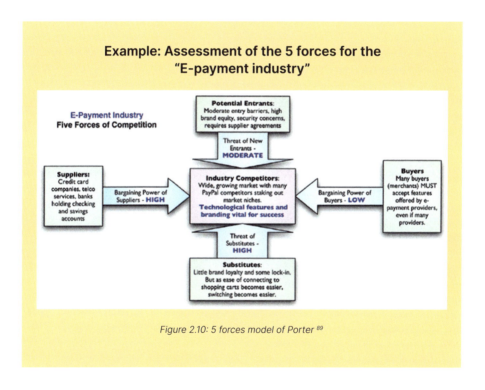

Figure 2.10: 5 forces model of Porter [89]

How to use the elements from this model for the main idea of **external analysis**:
- All elements coming from the Five Forces model of Porter, which are assessed as being **"high"**, can have a **"negative"** influence on the growth of the company, which need to be considered as **"Threats"**.
- All elements that are assessed as being **"low"**, might have a **"positive"** influence for the company and can lead to growth. So it can be considered as **"Opportunities"**.

Both elements will come together in the SWOT matrix, which will be explained in a further section.

Some extra information (related to the force "Buyer": Rogers' model)

The consumer model of Rogers, also known as the Diffusion of Innovations Theory, explains how, why, and at what rate new ideas and technology spread through cultures.

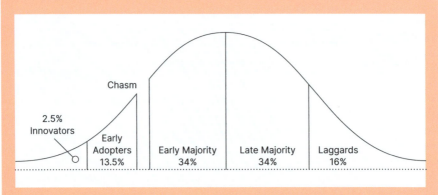

Figure 2.11: Rogers' consumer model [90]

Rogers categorises consumers into five adopter groups based on their readiness to adopt new innovations. Understanding these categories helps businesses target their marketing efforts more effectively.

1. **Innovators** (2.5% of the target population):
   <u>Characteristics</u>: Risk-takers, highly educated, have substantial financial resources, and are interested in new ideas and technologies.
   <u>Behaviour</u>: Eager to try new innovations, even if they come with risks. They play a crucial role in the introduction of new products.
2. **Early Adopters** (13.5%) (aka "trendsetters"):
   <u>Characteristics</u>: Social leaders, popular, educated, and have a higher social status.
   <u>Behaviour</u>: Embrace new ideas and innovations quickly but are more conscious and thoughtful than Innovators. They are often opinion leaders who influence the following groups.
3. **Early Majority** (34%):
   <u>Characteristics</u>: Average social status, critical before adopting new innovations, less risk-averse compared to the first two groups.
   <u>Behaviour</u>: Adopt innovations after a varying degree of time. They are typically the first significant group to adopt an innovation after some degree of market proof.
4. **Late Majority** (34%):
   <u>Characteristics</u>: Sceptical, lower social status, average financial liquidity, influenced by peer pressure.
   <u>Behaviour</u>: Adopt innovations after the average member of society. They need more proof and reassurance before adopting new products.
5. **Laggards** (16%):
   <u>Characteristics</u>: Traditional, conservative, (sometimes) lower social status, typically older and less financially fluid.
   <u>Behaviour</u>: Last to adopt an innovation. They rely on traditions and have little to no opinion leadership. They adopt new products when they are no longer seen as new and only when they become necessary.

When you plan to launch certain innovations or new ideas, you need to carefully analyse the situation you're in. This will be important for adapting some basic drivers of your plan:

A. Innovation itself:
   - Relative Advantage: The degree to which an innovation is perceived as better than the idea it supersedes.

Chapter 2: Strategic process

- Compatibility: How consistent the innovation is with the values, experiences, and needs of potential adopters.
- Complexity: How difficult the innovation is to understand and use.
- Trialability: The extent to which an innovation can be tested on a limited basis before making a full-scale commitment.

B. Communication Channels: The means by which information about an innovation is transmitted to members of a social system. This can include mass media, interpersonal channels, and digital platforms.

C. Time: The process by which an innovation is communicated over time among the participants in a social system.

The key "tipping point" in this journey is the so-called "chasm". The chasm represents a significant gap between two adopter groups: the early adopters and the early majority. This is a gap where many innovations fail to progress: while early adopters are excited about new technology, the early majority needs more convincing and proof of the product's viability and benefits.

To cross the chasm, businesses need to:

- Ensure the solution is reliable, user-friendly, and has demonstrable benefits.
- Provide evidence of successful implementations and satisfied customers among early adopters.
- Focus on niche markets where the product can dominate and then leverage this success to appeal to broader markets.

2.2.1.2 Strategic models (Porter / Treacy and Wiersema)

Another way to assess the "**external**" **MESO situation**, is by looking at the possible strategies that the competition pursue compared to your own business strategy. This will give you a serious hint about who exactly your direct competitor is and some insights on which direction to take in the future.

There are 2 interesting models that describe the strategy of a company:

- the model of Porter
- the model of Treacy and Wiersema

a. **Strategies model of Porter**

Besides its Five Forces Model, Michael Porter also established a framework to help business to position themselves effectively against competition: it's the so-called **Generic Strategies Model**.

For this model, Michael Porter uses 2 elements to build its framework:

a. On one hand, you have the "**competitive advantage**" with 2 possible options: working on "**costs**" or working on "**differentiation/distinctivity**".
b. On the other hand, you have the "**market scope**" with another 2 options: targeting the **entire market** or just a particular segment.

By doing so, you get a matrix, creating 3 major strategies:
1. **Cost Leadership**
2. **Differentiation**
3. **Focus (Cost or Differentiation)**

Figure 2.12: Strategy model of Porter [91]

Chapter 2: Strategic process

1. **Cost Leadership**
   Objective: Offer solutions to the whole market at the **lowest price** to attract price-sensitive customers.

   Characteristics of this strategy:
   a. Economies of scale
   b. Cost-saving technologies
   c. Efficient production processes
   d. Tight cost controls

   Examples of companies
   IKEA, Walmart, Colruyt, ...

2. **Differentiation**
   Objective: Charge a premium price for your solution to the whole market due to the perceived higher value.

   Characteristics of this strategy:
   a. Superior quality
   b. Innovative features
   c. Strong brand image
   d. Exceptional customer service

   Examples of companies
   Apple, BMW, Philips, ...

3. **Focus**
   Objective: Serve a particular group of customers/consumers better than competitors who target a broader audience.

   Sub-strategies
   Cost Focus: Targeting a specific market segment with the lowest cost.
   Differentiation Focus: Targeting a specific market segment with unique offerings.

   Characteristics of this strategy:
   a. Deep understanding of the target segment
   b. Tailored products or services to meet specific needs

c. Higher customer loyalty within the niche.

Examples of companies
Aldi (Cost focus) and Whole Foods / Bioplanet (Differentiation focus)

Remark: We consider Aldi to be "Cost focus" (and not cost leadership) as they target only price-sensitive consumers ... they don't look for the whole market offering a broad scale of products and brands.

Some companies have no exact idea which strategy to follow and they end up being "**Stuck in the middle**" of the whole framework. This situation is of course detrimental to survival in the long term.

b. **Strategies model of Treacy and Wiersema**
Another way to assess the different strategies on the market is the one developed by Treacy and Wiersema: the **Value Discipline Model**. They identified three primary value disciplines that companies can pursue to achieve market leadership, which are:
1. **Operational Excellence**
2. **Product Leadership**
3. **Customer Intimacy**

Figure 2.13: Strategy model of Treacy and Wiersema [92]

In order to become a leader in the market, you need to focus your strategy by maximising your value to your consumers by choosing one (or two) disciplines.

1. **Operational Excellence**
   Objective: Provide customers with reliable solutions at competitive prices with minimal inconvenience (aiming for the "**Best Total Cost**").

   Characteristics of this strategy:
   a. Streamlined operations
   b. Low-cost structure
   c. Consistent, reliable service
   d. High efficiency

Examples of companies

Examples of companies: IKEA, Walmart, Colruyt, ...

2. **Product Leadership**

   Objective: Offer the best product in the market, often commanding premium prices due to their advanced features and quality (aiming for the "**Best Product**").

   Characteristics of this strategy:
   a. Continuous innovation
   b. High-quality products
   c. Emphasis on research and development
   d. Strong brand image associated with innovation

   Examples of companies

   Examples of companies: Apple, BMW, Philips, ...

3. **Customer Intimacy**

   Objective: Develop a loyal customer base by exceeding customer expectations and providing personalised experiences (aiming for the "**Best Total Solution**").

   Characteristics of this strategy:
   a. Deep understanding of customer needs
   b. Customisation and personalisation of products or services
   c. Strong customer service and support
   d. Building long-term customer loyalty

   Examples of companies:

   Examples of companies: Netflix, Spotify, Ritz-Carlton, ...

Remark: While both Porter's models and Treacy and Wiersema's model are valuable in strategic management, they differ in their focus, scope, and application within the strategic decision-making process. Porter's models are about **industry analysis and competitive strategy**, whereas Treacy and Wiersema's model emphasises achieving market leadership through focused **value disciplines**.

2.2.1.3 Strategy matrices (BCG / GE)

The last models that can be used to assess the "**external**" **situation**, are the strategy matrices developed by certain companies:
- **Boston Consulting Group Matrix**
- **General Electric Matrix**

Both frameworks use the growth of market and product as the differentiating elements for a possible company's strategy.

Boston Consulting Group Matrix

The BCG (Boston Consulting Group) Matrix is a strategic business tool used to evaluate the relative performance of the company's **business units or product lines**. It helps in decision-making regarding resource allocation and strategic planning.

This framework uses 2 key elements:
1. **Market Growth Rate**: This axis represents the growth rate of the industry in which the business unit operates. A higher growth rate indicates a more dynamic and expanding market.
2. **Relative Market Share**: This axis represents the business unit's market share relative to its largest competitor. A higher relative market share suggests a stronger competitive position.

The matrix categorises business units into four quadrants based on their market growth rate and relative market share.

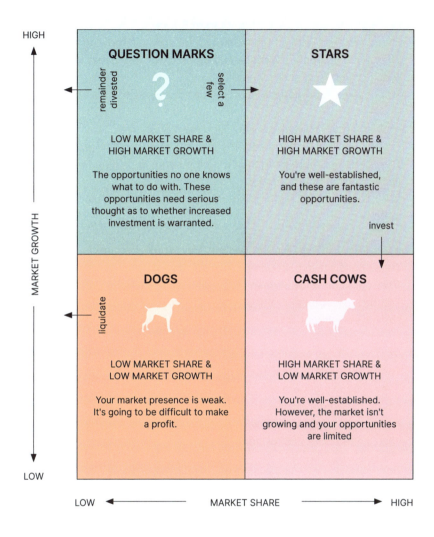

Figure 2.14: Strategy matrix of Boston Consulting Group (BCG) [93]

a. **Stars (High Market Growth, High Market Share)**
- These are units with a high market share in a fast-growing industry.
- They typically require **substantial investment** to sustain their growth and keep up with market demands.
- Stars have the potential to become cash cows as the market growth slows.

b. **Cash Cows (Low Market Growth, High Market Share)**
- These units have a high market share in a mature, slow-growing industry.
- They generate **more cash than they consume**, providing funds for the company to invest in other areas.
- Cash cows are crucial for maintaining profitability and funding other quadrants.

c. **Question Marks (High Market Growth, Low Market Share)**
- These units are in a growing market but hold a small market share.
- They consume **a lot of cash but do not generate much return**.
- The future potential is **uncertain**: they can either become stars with substantial investment or fail to gain significant market share and turn into dogs.

d. **Dogs (Low Market Growth, Low Market Share)**
- These units hold a small market share in a mature, slow-growing industry.
- They typically generate just enough cash to maintain themselves but are not considered a significant source of profit.
- Companies might consider divesting or discontinuing these units as they have limited potential for growth or profitability.

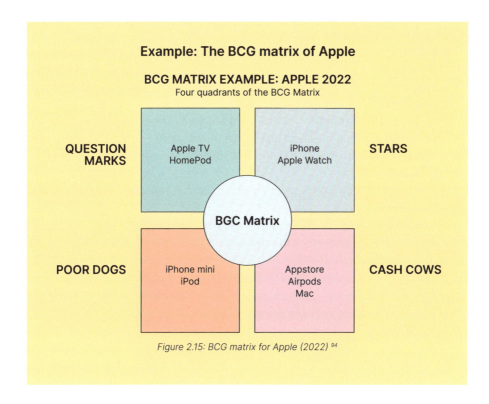

Figure 2.15: BCG matrix for Apple (2022) [94]

In general, the BCG matrix has the following guidelines as strategic implications:
1. **Invest in Stars** to maintain their position and support their growth.
2. **Harvest Cash Cows** to maximise cash flow with minimal investment.
3. **Evaluate Question Marks** to decide whether to invest heavily to increase market share or divest if the potential for growth is not viable.
4. **Divest or reposition Dogs** if they do not contribute significantly to the company's profitability or strategic goals.

General Electric Matrix
The GE (General Electric) Matrix, also known as the GE-McKinsey Matrix, is a strategic tool used to assess the **relative attractiveness of business units or product lines within a company**. This matrix is more sophisticated than the BCG Matrix as it considers multiple factors for evaluating industry attractiveness and business unit strength.

This framework uses 2 key elements:
1. **Industry Attractiveness**: This element evaluates the attractiveness of the industry in which the business unit operates. Factors include market size, market growth rate, profitability, competitive intensity, technological change, and regulatory environment.
2. **Business Unit Strength**: This element assesses the strength and competitive position of the business unit within the industry. Factors include market share, product quality, brand strength, distribution network, and R&D capabilities.

The matrix is a 3×3 grid, creating nine cells that represent different strategic options:
- Horizontal Axis (Business Unit Strength): high, medium, low.
- Vertical Axis (Industry Attractiveness): high, medium, low.

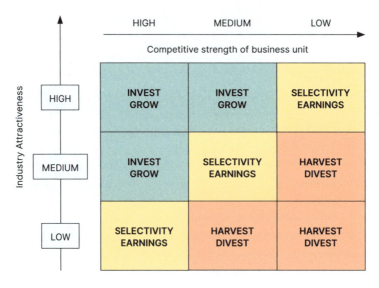

Figure 2.16: Strategy matrix of General Electric (GE) [95]

The matrix can be divided into **three main zones** for strategic decision-making:
1. **Grow (Green Zone):** Units in these cells are prime candidates for **investment** to grow market share, enhance competitive position, and capitalise on attractive market conditions.
2. **Hold (Yellow Zone):** Units in these cells should be maintained with a **focus** on **improving** their competitive position or **selectively investing** to strengthen their market standing.
3. **Harvest/Divest (Red Zone):** Units in these cells are candidates for **divestment** or **harvesting** (maximising short-term profits while minimising investment).

In general, the GE matrix has the following guidelines as strategic implications:
1. **Invest in High Attractiveness and Strong Business Units** to leverage their potential and secure a leading market position.
2. **Focus on Improving Business Units with Average Strength in Attractive Industries** to enhance their competitive position.
3. **Consider Divesting Units in Unattractive Industries with Weak Strength** to reallocate resources more effectively.

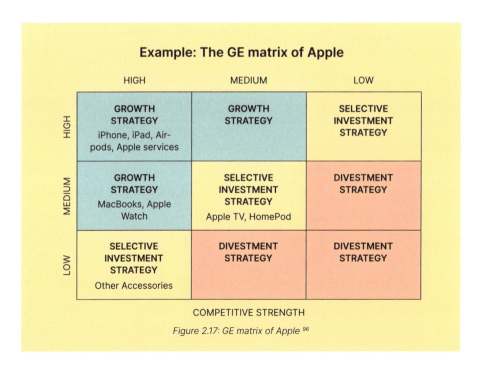

Figure 2.17: GE matrix of Apple [96]

2.2.1.4 General conclusion on Meso environment

In the previous sections, we described **several models** that can be used to assess the situation in the market. It allows us to gather all kinds of information around certain key elements to assess the **situation of a company** (providing a certain solution) **compared to the competition**.

All kinds of data that come out of the analyses of the different Meso models can be gathered in a simple "competition" overview sheet that can be used to analyse the overall situation in the market. An example can be found just below.

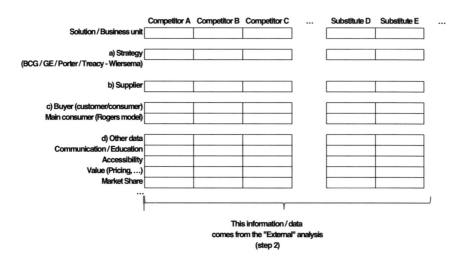

Figure 2.18: Overview sheet of the MESO environment

Using this assessment sheet will help you to filter the possible "Opportunities" and "Threats".
- All elements that are considered "**strong**" on the competition side can have a "**negative**" influence on the growth of the company. These need to be considered as "**Threats**".
- All elements that are considered "**weak**" on the competition side can have a "**positive**" influence on the growth of the company. These need to be considered as "**Opportunities**".

2.2.2 External analysis: Macro environment

Besides analysing the direct market (= Meso environment), you also need to evaluate **the overall trends which involve all organisations on this planet (= Macro environment**). You can distinguish both local and global tendencies. The easiest way to capture the most relevant trends for your company is by using the DESTEP or PESTLE models.

MODELS TO ANALYSE THE "MACRO" ENVIRONMENT

a. DESTEP (or PESTLE)

Figure 2.19: Model to analyse MACRO environment (External analysis)

2.2.2.1 DESTEP (or PESTLE)

The DESTEP & PESTLE models are strategic tools used for analysing the external environment and its potential impact on an organisation.

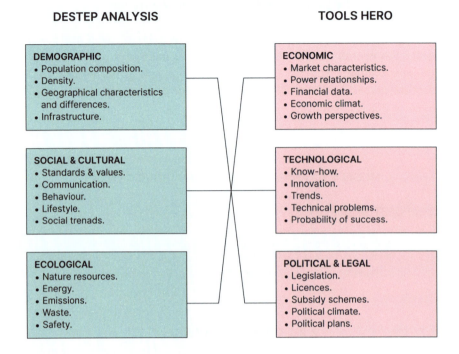

Figure 2.20: DESTEP model in detail [97]

DESTEP stands for the following trends:
Demographic
Examples of underlying factors:
- Population size and growth
- Age distribution
- Geographical distribution
- Household composition
- Education levels
- ...

Economic
Examples of underlying factors:
- Economic growth
- Inflation rates

- Employment rates
- Interest rates
- Exchange rates
- ...

Socio-cultural

Examples of underlying factors:
- Cultural trends and norms
- Lifestyle changes
- Education levels
- Attitudes towards work and leisure
- Social mobility
- ...

Technological

Examples of underlying factors:
- Innovation and R&D
- Automation and AI
- Communication technologies
- Access to technology
- ...

Ecological

Examples of underlying factors:
- Environmental regulations
- Climate change
- Sustainability trends
- Natural resources
- Waste management
- ...

Political

Examples of underlying factors:
- Government stability
- Regulatory environment
- Trade policies
- Tax policies
- Lobbying and advocacy
- ...

Assessing this model will help you to find out which trends are possible "Opportunities" and "Threats".

- All trends that might threaten your situation that will lead to "**negative**" influence on the growth of the company. These need to be considered as "**Threats**".
- All trends that might sustain your situation which will lead to a "**positive**" influence on the growth of the company. These need to be considered as "**Opportunities**".

Remark: In certain areas, we don't use the DESTEP model although it's called the PESTLE model. PESTLE is the abbreviation for this list of trends:

- Political
- Economic
- Social
- Technological
- Legal
- Environmental

Both models have a lot in common, although there are 2 small differences:
- The DESTEP model includes Demographic factors as a distinct category, whereas the PESTLE model integrates these aspects within the broader Social factors.
- On the other hand, PESTLE distinguishes the Legal as a separate factor, besides the Political one. In the DESTEP model the Legal factor is included under the Political part.

2.3 Step 3: Internal analysis

Starting with external analysis helps a company understand market trends, customer needs, and competition first, thereby avoiding the danger of assuming everything is going well without considering external realities. This knowledge informs how the company assesses its own strengths and weaknesses later. It ensures that strategies are relevant, opportunities are identified early, and potential threats are anticipated and addressed proactively, even when things appear to be going smoothly internally.

In the previous sections, we've explained the external situation, being the Meso- and Macro-environment. To finalise this exercise, we also need to investigate the "internal" situation within the company itself, aka the Micro environment.

2.3.1 Internal analysis: Micro environment

Referring back to the introduction of section 2.3, the internal analysis focuses on the first environment (Micro). By researching the situation in the company itself, you will find information (data) that will be categorised as "Strengths" or "Weaknesses":
- "**Strengths**" are elements from Micro that might help the company to grow (positive effect)
- "**Weaknesses**" are elements from Micro that might push the company to losses (negative effect)

There are certain models that will help us to analyse the Micro area:
- Value Chain model by Porter
- 7S model of McKinsey

MODELS TO ANALYSE THE "MICRO" ENVIRONMENT

a. **Value chain model** by Porter
b. **7S model** by McKinsey

Figure 2.21: Different models to analyse MICRO environment (Internal analysis)

2.3.1.1 Value Chain model by Porter

The Value Chain model, developed by Michael Porter, is a strategic tool used to analyse the specific activities through which firms can create value and gain a competitive advantage. It's used to analyse the internal situation of a company. The model breaks down the company into primary and support activities that contribute to the overall value creation process.

Chapter 2: Strategic process

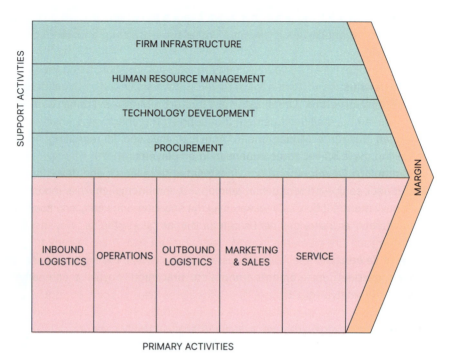

Figure 2.22: Value Chain model (by Porter) [98]

Primary Activities:
1. **Inbound Logistics**: Activities related to receiving, storing, and inputs for the solution, such as material handling, warehousing, inventory control, and transportation.
2. **Operations**: Activities that transform inputs into finished solution (products, services, ...), including machining, packaging, assembly, equipment maintenance, and testing.
3. **Outbound Logistics**: Activities involved in distributing the final solution to customers, such as warehousing, order fulfilment, transportation, and distribution management.
4. **Marketing and Sales**: Activities aimed at attracting customers and selling products, including advertising, promotion, sales force, channel selection, pricing, and managing relationships with distributors and retailers.

5. **Service**: Activities that maintain and enhance the product's value, such as customer support, repair services, installation, training, and product upgrades.

Support Activities:
1. **Firm Infrastructure**: Organisational structure, control systems, company culture, and overall management that support the entire value chain.
2. **Human Resource Management**: Activities involved in recruiting, hiring, training, developing, and compensating employees.
3. **Technology Development**: Activities related to research and development, product design, process development, and technology improvements.
4. **Procurement**: Activities involved in acquiring raw materials, components, equipment, and services necessary for the firm's operations.

The goal of value chain analysis is to identify areas **where the firm can improve efficiency, reduce costs, or differentiate its products** to gain a competitive advantage. By analysing each activity, businesses can pinpoint **strengths** and **weaknesses**, optimise processes, and enhance the overall value delivered to customers.

Example: The value chain model of Amazon

SUPPORT ACTIVITIES	**FIRM INFRASTRUCTURE:** Company's support system and the functions that allow it to maintain operations. Includes all legal, administrative and accounting.	
	HUMAN RESOURCES: Hiring and retaining employees who will fulfill business strategy, as well as help design, market, and sell product. Involve the process of delivering the finished product. A source of competitive advantage when customer purchasing a service.	
	TECHNOLOGY: Research and development helps designing the product and improving and automating the process. For example, a business working towards reducing the inventory and labour waste by implementing RFID technology in warehouse to improve overall stock accuracy and minimise labour tasks.	
	PROCUREMENT: Process of acquisition of inputs, raw materials, or resources, for the firm. This relates heavily to inbound logistics where the company is looking to resale the goods they procure. For example, in the case of an e-commerce business.	

	INBOUND LOGISTICS:	PRODUCTION/ OPERATIONS:	OUTBOUND LOGISTICS:	MARKETING & SALES:	CUSTOMER SERVICE:	
PRIMARY ACTIVITIES	Amazon sources products from suppliers around the world and transports them to fulfillment centres. Advanced logistics and inventory management systems optimise its inbound logistics and ensure that products are available for sale in a timely manner.	Orders are processed and prepared for shipment through Amazon's fullfillment centres. The company utilises advanced automataion technologies and robotics to streamline its operations and improve efficiency and reduce labour costs.	Amazon ships products to customers around the world using a network of carriers and logistic partners. It provides fast and convenient service through a range of delivery options.	Its website, mobile app, and social media platforms give Amazon a variety of ways to reach customers. The company offers personalised product recommendations and targeted advertising to enhance the customer experience.	Amazon places a strong emphasis on providing high-quality customer service, including fast and easy returns, 24/7 customer support, and a range of self-service options. Amazon Prime is a loyalty programme that provides customers with free shipping, exclusive discounts, and other benefits in addition to supplying the company with more revenue.	**MARGIN**

Figure 2.23: Value chain of Amazon [99]

2.3.1.2. 7S model of McKinsey

Another model that can be used to assess the "internal" situation is the so-called "7S" model elaborated by the consultancy firm McKinsey & Company. This framework emphasises the **interconnectedness of seven key elements that need to be aligned for an organisation to be effective**. These elements are categorised as "**hard**" and "**soft**" elements.

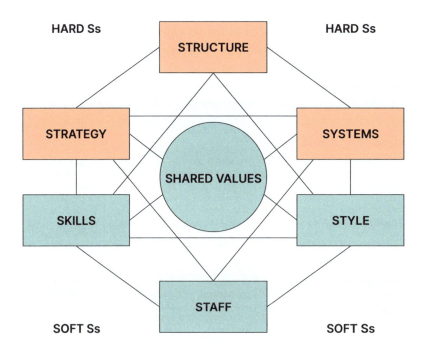

Figure 2.24: 7S model (by McKinsey) [100]

Hard Elements:
- **Strategy**: The plan devised to maintain and build competitive advantage over the competition. It includes the organisation's vision, mission, and strategic goals (see above).
- **Structure**: The organisational chart and the division of labour. It defines how tasks are divided, coordinated, and supervised.

- **Systems**: The daily activities and procedures that staff use to get the job done. These include both **formal** and **informal** processes and information flows.

Soft Elements:
- **Shared Values**: The core values and fundamental beliefs that guide the organisation's actions and behaviour. Shared values are central to the model and serve as the **foundation** for the other elements.
- **Style**: The **leadership approach** and **management style**. It reflects how key managers behave in achieving the organisation's goals and how they interact with employees.
- **Staff**: The employees and their general **capabilities**. This element focuses on people, their backgrounds, competencies, and how the organisation recruits, trains, and motivates them.
- **Skills**: The actual **skills** and **competencies** of the employees working within the organisation. It looks at what the organisation does best and the capabilities and talents present within it.

The 7S Model emphasises that all seven elements are interconnected and a change in one element will affect the others.

For example, a change in strategy (hard element) will likely require changes in systems, skills, and possibly shared values (soft elements) to be effective.

Therefore, the model is often used for organisational change management, diagnosing issues (where are the "**strengths**" and "**weaknesses**"?), or aligning elements for optimal performance.

Example: The 7S model for McDonald's

MCDONALD'S EFFECTIVELY APPLIES MCKINSEY'S 7S-MODEL

- STRATEGY: Cost-cutting approach and SMART objectives.
- STRUCTURE: Flat organisation with accessible top management.

- SYSTEMS: Innovations to enhance production efficiency, like the McDonald's app and self-ordering kiosks.
- SHARED VALUES: Emphasising integrity, diversity, collaboration, and community support.
- STYLE: Participatory leadership style with employee feedback.
- STAFF: Fostering employee happiness and embracing diversity.
- SKILLS: Training for exceptional customer service and conflict resolution.

Figure 2.25: 7S model of McDonalds [101]

Some extra information: The PLC model (Product Life Cycle)

The Product Life Cycle model describes the stages a product goes through from its inception to its decline and eventual withdrawal from the market. Understanding the PLC helps companies manage their products more effectively and make strategic decisions.

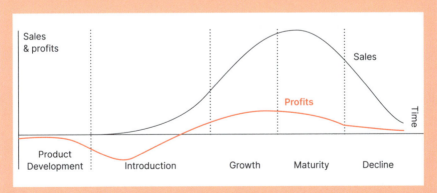

Figure 2.26: PLC model [102]

Chapter 2: Strategic process

We can distinguish the following stages in the PLC model:

Product Development:
- Development: The solution is developed.
- Costs: Only development costs.
- Profit: Decreasing as there's no sales at this moment.

Introduction:
- Product Launch: The product is introduced to the market.
- Marketing Efforts: High investment in advertising and promotions to build awareness.
- Sales Growth: Initial sales may be slow as the market learns about the product.
- Costs: High development and marketing costs.
- Profit: Improves with the growth in sales.

Growth:
- Market Acceptance: Sales begin to increase rapidly as more customers become aware of and start buying the product.
- Competition: Competitors may enter the market with similar products.
- Marketing Strategy: Focus shifts to differentiating the product from competitors and expanding market share.
- Profit: The product starts generating profits as sales volume increases.

Maturity:
- Peak Sales: Sales growth slows as the product reaches peak market penetration.
- Market Saturation: Most potential customers have bought the product.
- Price Competition: Increased competition may lead to price reductions.
- Product Updates: Companies may introduce new features or improvements to rejuvenate the product.
- Profit: Profit margins may start to decline due to increased competition and market saturation.

Decline:
- Decreasing Sales: Sales begin to fall as the product becomes outdated or market conditions change.
- Profit: Profits decrease as sales decline and the product becomes less relevant. (Remark: Sometimes, you can decide to cash out this solution by increasing the price, which will lead to a short-term profit boost.)

- Possible decisions:
  a. Market Exit: Companies may phase out the product, stop production, and withdraw it from the market.
  b. Divestment: Focus may shift to other more profitable products or new innovations ("rejuvenation").

During each stage of the PLC model, you need to act differently as a marketer:
1. **Introduction**: During this phase, you will invest in marketing means to educate potential consumers and create awareness. You need to focus on quality and differentiation, to establish a strong presence.
2. **Growth**: Once in the growth phase, you need to expand distribution and enhance features/variants to attract more customers. It's actually the stage when competition is entering the market. As of pricing, you will need to start balancing between gaining market share and maintaining profitability.
3. **Maturity**: The maturity stage is the one characterised by fierce competition battles. So you will streamline operations to maintain profitability and will start strong promotional activities to steal consumers from competitors. Moreover, you will also start targeting specific customer segments with tailored marketing strategies.
4. **Decline**: The final stage of the PLC is forcing marketeers to reduce costs to maintain profitability as sales decline. You will need to decide to discontinue unprofitable variations and start planning for the future: investing in new products to replace the declining ones.

Based on this PLC model, you can evaluate what stage your solution and the ones from your competitors are in and what the future might be for them, deciding if the situation is "relatively" positive (= strength) or negative (= weakness).

2.3.1.3 General conclusion on Micro environment

In the previous sections, we've described several models that can be used to assess the **internal situation within the company**. This analysis is very complementary to the one explained in "step 2" (external analysis).

All kinds of data that come out of the analyses of the different Micro models can be uploaded on the "competition" overview sheet used in the previous step. This way, you can assess the internal situation vs the competition.

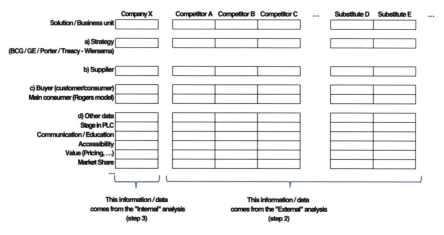

Figure 2.27: Overview sheet of the MICRO and MESO environment

Using this sheet will help you to filter the possible "Strengths" and "Weaknesses".
- All elements that are considered "**strong**" at company side can have a "**positive**" influence on the growth of the company itself. These need to be considered as "**Strengths**".
- All elements that are considered "**weak**" at company side can have a "**negative**" influence on the growth of the company. These need to be considered as "**Weaknesses**".

2.4 Step 4: SWOT: the ultimate summary

Once you've finished the external and the internal analysis, you can put all elements together in the SWOT matrix: SWOT stands for "Strengths", "Weaknesses", "Opportunities" and "Threats" (see previous chapters).

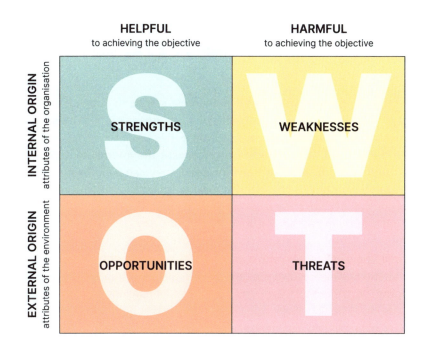

Figure 2.28: SWOT analysis [103]

It's important to remember 2 basic elements from the matrix:
a. **Fact no 1:**
Strengths and Opportunities are "**positive**" elements that can help to grow your business.
Weaknesses and Threats are "**negative**" elements that can impact your business.

b. Fact no 2:
Strengths and Weaknesses are derived from the "internal" analysis (step 3).
Opportunities and Threats are derived from the "external" analysis (step 2).

Very important: Both strengths and weaknesses as opportunities and threats are clear interpretations based on **facts and data** coming from the internal and external analysis. **These never reflect future aspirations** and can never be written this way (for example by using verbs like "will", "may", "can", ...).

2.5 Step 5: Going from strategic to operational marketing

After completing your SWOT analysis, the next step is to find ways that might leverage your strengths and opportunities to address your weaknesses. Since weaknesses are the most critical elements in this process, it's essential to focus on these areas first. **Weaknesses represent the internal factors that can hinder your success, and if left unaddressed, they can become major barriers to achieving your goals.** These might include limitations in skills, resources, or processes that put you at a competitive disadvantage. Don't forget... the competition will also try to "hit" you on your weaknesses...

By prioritising weaknesses, you can identify the specific areas that need immediate attention. Once you've identified them, the next step is to leverage your **strengths** – whether that's expertise, resources, or relationships – to minimise or eliminate these weaknesses. Additionally, external **opportunities** should be explored to help mitigate weaknesses, such as trends in the market, technological advancements, or potential partnerships. The key to overcoming weaknesses lies in developing concrete action plans.

Finally, continuous monitoring and adaptation are essential. Weaknesses can evolve, and new challenges may arise. Regularly evaluating your progress will help you stay agile and adjust your strategies to remain on track.

In summary, you're coming to the point of betting on the right strategic option(s) to get the best result for your company/brand.

Example: Kodak Case

Figure 2.29: Kodak instant camera [104]

The Kodak case is a classic example of how weaknesses can hinder a company's success, even when it has a dominant market position. Kodak, once the leader in the photography industry, failed to adapt to the digital revolution. Its primary weakness was its resistance to change and reliance on its traditional film-based business model, despite early warning signs of the growing digital photography market.

Kodak had the technology to develop digital cameras and imaging systems but was hesitant to fully embrace it, fearing it would cannibalise their profitable film sales. This reluctance to innovate and pivot towards digital photography was a significant weakness. Additionally, Kodak's strong brand and history in traditional film photography led to complacency, causing them to underestimate the rapid technological shifts occurring in the industry.

As a result, Kodak missed out on the digital camera boom, and by the time they attempted to shift focus, competitors like Canon, Sony, and Nikon had already established themselves in the digital space. Kodak's failure to address these weaknesses, especially its slow adaptation to digital trends, ultimately led to its decline and bankruptcy filing in 2012.

2.5.1 Strategic options

Combine different elements of SWOT to create strategies that leverage strengths and opportunities, address weaknesses, and mitigate threats. You have the following combinations:

- **Strengths-Opportunities (SO) Strategies**: Use your strengths to take advantage of opportunities.
- **Weaknesses-Opportunities (WO) Strategies**: Overcome weaknesses by exploiting opportunities.
- **Weaknesses-Threats (WT) Strategies**: Minimise weaknesses and defend against threats.

	STRENGTHS Positive characteristics and advantages of the issue, situation, or technique.	**WEAKNESSES** Negative characteristics and disadvantages of the issue, situation, or technique.
OPPORTUNITIES Factors, situations that can benefit, enhance or improve the issue, situation or technique.	**S-O STRATEGY/ ANALYSIS** Using strengths to take advantage of opportunities.	**W-O STRATEGY/ ANALYSIS** Overcoming weaknesses by taking advantage of opportunities.
THREATS Factors, situations that can hinder the issue, situation, or technique.	**S-T STRATEGY/ ANALYSIS** Using strengths to avod threats.	**W-T STRATEGY/ ANALYSIS** Minimise weaknesses and aviod threats.

Figure 2.30: Strategic Options [105]

These strategies that are distilled from the SWOT matrix are also called "Strategic options".

Let's make it concrete with the following example.

188   Marketing

Example: Fictitious SWOT

STRENGTHS	WEAKNESSES
• Solution X has a gross profitability of 40%. • Solution X is only made of natural ingredients.	• The brand awareness level in Belgium is only 20% within our target group. • We have no strategy for the coming 3 years.
OPPORTUNITIES	**THREATS**
• We have no distribution in The Netherlands. • People are buying more sustainable products.	• Competition A will launch a 100% natural product next year. • The inflation rate remains high: 5% year-on-year

Figure 2.31: SWOT solution X

In the next step, you can try to look at the possibilities of how the current strengths and opportunities can be used to tackle the existing weaknesses and threats. This can be done by putting the strengths and weaknesses at the top of a table and the opportunities and threats on the left side. Then, you need to assess each strategy that is possible (S-O / S-T / W-O / W-T) and see how they might impact each other: **a big (positive/negative) impact is set as "++" or "- -" , a limited (positive/negative) impact is set as "+" or "-". No possible impact leaves the strategy "blank".**

In our example above, you can assess it in the following way:

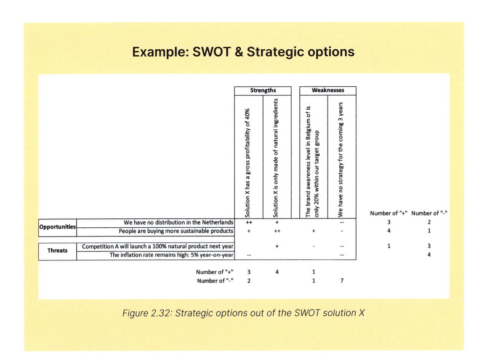

Figure 2.32: Strategic options out of the SWOT solution X

Now, it's important to choose the elements that have the biggest impact on the situation, meaning getting more growth or avoiding big problems. This can be done by looking at the number of "+" and "-" for each SWOT element.
Let's analyse the most important SWOT elements:
- Most important strength = "the natural ingredients" (4x "+")
- Most important weakness = "no strategy" (7x "-")
- Most important opportunity = "People are buying sustainable"
- Most important threat = "inflation rate"

Example: Elaborated Strategic options

Knowing this, you can distil the 2 biggest "strategic options":

a. **Focusing your communication** on the natural ingredients which will have an impact on the awareness level of people who want to buy more sustainably.

b. **Building a long-term strategy** that will avoid problems with the inflation trend, looking at possible projects for the longer term (communication, export, ...) and secure your position in the market.

Not all strategic options can be implemented at once. That's why you need to prioritise them based on:

a. **Impact**: The potential positive effect on the business.

b. **Feasibility**: The practicality of implementation given current resources and constraints.

c. **Urgency**: The immediacy of the need to address specific issues or capitalise on opportunities.

This can be done by the management and marketing team, by scoring each strategic option out of 10 on impact, feasibility, and urgency.

Let's go back to our example above...

Example: Fictitious SWOT

	IMPACT (/10)	FEASIBILITY (/10)	URGENCY (/10)	TOTAL (/30)
STRATEGIC OPTION 1: Communication	8	6	7	21
STRATEGIC OPTION 2: Strategy	5	9	9	23

Figure 2.33: Evaluation of Strategic options

The "strategy" option will have a limited short-term impact, though it doesn't cost you a lot of money and time and considering the situation on the market, it might be very useful to have it.

The "communication" option will have a higher short-term impact, but it might require some budget. That's why we assess it at the moment as less urgent.

This means we put a higher priority on the "strategy" option, though considering the small difference between the 2 strategic options, it might be useful to do this exercise again after a couple of months to see if the situation has changed (and that other options might be preferable).

Remark 1: In the dynamic world of business, it's crucial to conduct regular SWOT analyses to stay ahead of the curve. What was considered a strength a year ago might no longer be a competitive advantage today. Similarly, new opportunities can emerge, and previously identified threats may become more pressing. **Regular SWOT analyses** allow companies to reassess and realign their strategies, ensuring they capitalise on their strengths, address their weaknesses, seize new opportunities, and mitigate potential threats.

Remark 2: Sometimes you can combine certain "strategic" options to tackle several opportunities at once. In the described example, you can add the "sustainable" element as one of the key items in your strategy. This way, you can optimise your marketing strategy, which will lead to better results.

Some extra information: SFA-model

There's another model that can be used to evaluate the different strategic options. It's the so-called "**SFA-model**", developed by Johnson and Scholes. The SFA Model stands for **Suitability**, **Feasibility**, and **Acceptability**. Here's an accurate description of each component:

1. **Suitability**: Suitability assesses whether a particular strategic option is aligned with the organisation's goals, objectives, and external environment. It looks at how well the strategy fits with the current situation of the company.

   Key questions to ask here:
   - Does the strategy align with the organisation's long-term objectives and goals?
   - Is it appropriate for the current market conditions and the competitive environment?
   - Does the option take advantage of the organisation's strengths and opportunities?

2. **Feasibility**: Feasibility evaluates whether the organisation has the resources and capabilities to successfully implement the strategy. This involves considering the financial, operational, and human resources needed to execute the plan.

   Key questions to ask during this phase include:
   - Do we have the financial resources to support the strategy?
   - Can we execute the strategy within the required timeframe?
   - Do we have the necessary skills, expertise, and work force?
   - Are there any operational or technological constraints that could hinder implementation?

3. **Acceptability**: Acceptability assesses whether the strategic option is acceptable to key stakeholders, including shareholders, employees, customers, and other external parties. This involves understanding the risk-return balance and determining whether the strategy aligns with stakeholder expectations.

   Key questions to consider:
   - What are the financial implications of the strategy (e.g. expected profits, ROI)?
   - What are the risks involved, and are they acceptable to stakeholders?
   - Will the strategy be acceptable to employees, customers, or regulatory bodies?

- Does the strategy meet the interests and expectations of shareholders or other key stakeholders?

Here's a (fictitious) example of this SFA-matrix

PERSPECTIVE	WEIGHTING	OPTION 1	OPTION 2	OPTION 3
SUITABILITY	7,0			
Does it solve the main problem?	3	8	3	8
Does it exploit strengths and opportunities?	2	5	4	6
Does it minimise weaknesses and threats?	2	7	7	8
FEASABILITY	22,0			
Are there enough financial resources?	5	8	8	3
Is it organisationally achievable?	4	9	6	6
Is it economically justifiable?	2	6	8	7
Is it technologically achievable?	3	4	3	8
Is it socially acceptable?	5	8	7	9
Is it legally justifiable?	2	4	8	4
Is it ecologically acceptable?	1	5	9	7
ACCEPTABILITY	9,0			
Is it profitable?	4	6	3	8
Is there a financial risk?	2	8	7	4
Is it accepted by stakeholders?	3	3	8	6
TOTAL		250	230	247

Figure 2.34: SFA Matrix [106]

For the evaluation, you can give a certain "weight" to the different SFA elements. The use of weighting in the SFA (Suitability, Feasibility, Acceptability) model is important because not all of the three elements may be equally important in every situation. Weighting helps prioritise certain criteria that are more critical for the specific strategic decision at hand.

In the table above, it's clear that Option 1 is the best option to pursue.

2.5.2 Optimising value

Once you have chosen a certain "strategic option", you will need to make the **translation** of it to some key elements of your company. You need to check if your choice has any **impact** on:
- **strategic overview (mission, vision, strategic goals, values)**
- **strategy & target group (customer & consumer)**
- **value proposition (SAVE)**

2.5.2.1 (New) Strategic overview

Pursuing new "strategic options" might impact your strategy, explained in Step 1. As mentioned, you will need to assess if your "options" might ask you to change the strategic direction you're following:
a. **Change in mission**: are we still completely doing "what" we were doing before or do we need to adapt our mission statement?
b. **Change in vision**: are we still reaching the long-term objectives ("where are we heading to"?) or do we need to (slightly) adapt our vision?
c. **Change in strategic goals**: are the "strategic options" in line with the strategic goals we've developed to reach our long-term objective? Can we find some ground in the strategic goals for our chosen options?
d. **Change in values**: and what about our value statements... do they match our chosen "strategic options" or do we need to refine our internal core?

It's clear that the "SWOT" analysis is an exercise that needs to be done on a regular basis and it will depict a clear picture of the "reason of being" of the organisation in the long term. Once convinced about the "strategic" elements, you can pursue the planning exercise to work out your strategic options into tactical actions, leading to your operational marketing plan (SAVE model).

2.5.2.2 (New) Target group:
Segmentation – Targeting – Positioning

Once you have chosen for certain "strategic options", you need to think about the **optimal target groups** and how to reach them in order to maximise results. This exercise is known as the STP model, standing for "Segmentation – Targeting – Positioning", which was elaborated in detail in the first part of this book.

2.5.2.3 (New) Value proposition – (New) SAVE

In the previous steps, you have checked if the pursued strategy needs to be updated and if there are any changes on the target group and the concrete positioning of your "updated" solution.

After having processed all previous "strategic" steps, it's important to translate the "new" adopted strategic option **into the tactics and operational activities**, structured by the SAVE model. In other words, **you will try to describe the chosen strategic option in concrete action**s in the following areas:
- **Solution**: do you need to change certain elements in your offer to maximise value, based on your findings on the chosen target group and positioning?
- **Access**: do you need to adapt your Customer Journey?
- **Value**: is your value "optimal" or do you think you're missing certain actions to improve your value?
- **Education**: and how will you educate your target group: what actions are needed to communicate your solution to the target group with the desired positioning?

More details about the SAVE model, can be found in the first part of this book (Part 1: Operational marketing).

It's obvious that you make the actions very concrete with clear Key Performance Indicators (KPIs) in order to check if the results of your actions are in line with your strategic option. Actually, these results will be the base for the yearly strategic analysis and lead you back to step 1 of this Strategic Planning Process.

2.6 Overview on "strategic planning"

Strategic planning is a step-by-step process which will help you to choose the best strategic options given the situation both "externally" and "internally".

Step 1: Strategic overview
- Mission
- Vision
- Strategic objectives/Goals
- Values

Step 2: External analysis
- MESO environment
- 5 Forces Model (Porter)
- Strategic Models (Porter & Treacy/Wiersema)
- Strategic Matrices (BCG & GE)
- MACRO environment
- DESTEP

Step 3: Internal analysis
- MICRO environment
- Value Chain (Porter)
- 7S Model (Mc Kinsey)

Step 4: SWOT analysis

Step 5: Strategic options (going from strategy to operational)
- Confrontation Matrix
- Evaluation of the options
- Impact on Strategy, Target (STP) and Value (SAVE)

Epilogue:
The future of Marketing is built on
Trust and Value

As we look ahead, it's clear that the marketing landscape will continue to evolve at a rapid pace. New technologies will emerge, customer expectations will shift, and the world will become even more interconnected. But one thing remains constant: the importance of value. In the end, it's the value you offer your customers that will determine your success, not just the products you sell or the prices you set.

Marketing, at its core, has always been about creating connections. But in this new era, those connections must be built on trust. Trust is the foundation of the customer journey – it is what makes a customer choose you over the competition, stay loyal to your brand, and become an advocate for your business. Trust is not built overnight; it is earned through consistent value, transparent communication, and a genuine commitment to improving the lives of your customers.

As you move forward in your marketing journey, remember that the most successful brands are those that prioritise customer relationships over transactions. They understand that marketing is no longer a one-way street; it's a conversation, a relationship that evolves over time. In this evolving digital world, the companies that will thrive are those that adapt, embrace change, and focus on creating value at every touchpoint.

The tools and models we've explored in this book – whether through the operational lens of the SAVE model or the strategic insights of the customer decision journey – are just the beginning. These frameworks provide the structure, but it's the trust you build with your customers that will guide you through the complexities of the modern marketing world. Value isn't just what you deliver – it's what your customers experience, believe in, and ultimately rely on as they navigate their own journeys with your brand.

So, as you step forward, challenge yourself to think beyond products, beyond price, beyond the traditional norms. Focus on building genuine value that resonates with your customers' needs and aspirations. Create experiences that foster trust, encourage loyalty, and inspire advocacy. This is how lasting brands are built – not just through transactions, but through relationships rooted in trust and meaningful value.

The future of marketing is not about competing for attention – it's about earning and nurturing trust. And as long as you remain committed to delivering value, the path ahead will be filled with opportunity, growth, and success.

Acknowledgements

The creation of this marketing handbook has been a journey filled with learning, growth, and collaboration. I am deeply grateful to the people who have supported and inspired me along the way.

First, to my students, thank you for your enthusiasm, curiosity, and willingness to engage with new ideas. Your questions, insights, and feedback have continually challenged me to refine my thinking and keep pushing the boundaries of what I teach. Your dedication and eagerness to learn have been a constant source of motivation throughout this process.

To my fellow teachers and colleagues, I extend my heartfelt thanks. The exchange of knowledge and experiences within our community has enriched my own understanding of the subject matter and kept me inspired to create a resource that will be useful to others.

I would also like to express my sincere appreciation to my publisher, Lannoo and Lannoocampus. Your belief in this project and your professional guidance have made this book possible. I am grateful for your expertise in bringing this work to life. Finally, to my family, words cannot express how much your love and encouragement have meant to me. To my wife, Karolien, and my daughters Estelle and Elise. Your unwavering support and understanding have been my foundation throughout this project. This book is as much a product of your love as it is of my hard work.

Thank you all for being a part of this incredible journey.

1   Kotler, P. (1997) Marketing Management: Analysis, Planning, Implementation, and Control. Prentice Hall.

2   Dávila Sáenz, A. (2014). Re-inventando las 4P del Marketing al SAVE. Marketeros LATAM. https://www.marketeroslatam.com/wp-content/uploads/2014/05/de-las-4p-al-save.jpg

3   Ettenson, R., Conrado, E. & Knowles, J. (2013). Rethinking the 4P's. *Harvard Business Review.*

4   Acutt, M. S.A.V.E Marketing - Update To The 4P's & 7P's. https://marketingmix.co.uk/save-marketing/

5   Kahneman, D. (2015). *Thinking Fast and Slow. It enables you to make better decisions.* Penguin Books Ltd.

6   Carroll, L. (2018). Better decisions: two systems. Medium. https://uxdesign.cc/better-decisions-72e955c70a5c

7   Maslow, A. H. (1943). A theory of human motivation. *Psychological Review.*

8   NiceDay. (n.d.). *Pyramid of Maslow* [Figure]. NiceDay.

9   ResearchGate. (n.d.). *The ten most valuable companies from 1995 to 2018* [Figure]. ResearchGate. https://www.researchgate.net/figure/The-ten-most-valuable-companies-from-1995-to-2018-by-marketcapitalization-in-billion-US_fig1_349964525

10 Credits:ilbusca. Stockfoto ID:171327089

11 Credits:track5. Stock photo ID:458517521

12 Credits: Wirestock. Stock photo ID:1439134430

13 Credit: Sundry Photography. Stock photo ID:1068485000

14 Credit: gorodenkoff. Stock photo ID:1460765605

15 Sanchez, V. (2023). The origin and evolution of Chat GPT: The natural language model that is changing the game. RoutineHub Blog. https://blog.routinehub.co/content/images/size/w2000/2023/02/openAI-chat-gpt-1.jpg

16 Praxie. (n.d.). Kotler's Five Product Levels Model. https://praxie.com/kotlers-five-product-levels-model-online-tools-templates/

17 Toolshero. (n.d.). Kotler's Five Product Levels Model [Figure]. Toolshero. https://www.slidesalad.com/wp-content/uploads/2020/06/Kotler-Five-Product-Levels-PowerPoint-Templates-Model-0003.jpg

18 Hawker, K. (n.d.). Keller's Brand Equity Model: What It Is & How to Use It. Medium. https://medium.com/@keatonhawker/kellers-brand-equity-model-what-it-is-how-to-use-it-84e42d562299

19 alexbrandmanagement. (2013). Keller's Brand Equity Model. Wordpress.

20 Kapferer, J.-N. (2012). The new strategic brand management: Advanced insights and strategic thinking.

21 https://www.batheories.com/wp-content/uploads/brand-identity-prism-kapferer.png

22 https://brandalfblog.com/wp-content/uploads/2021/03/BN-1-1536×1081.png

23 https://www.yieldify.com/wp-content/uploads/2020/09/stp-model-segmentation-23 targeting-positioning.webp

24 https://qualaroo.com/blog/wp-content/uploads/2023/05/Types-of-Market-Segmentation-1.webp

25 Mora, M. (2021). Segmentation vs. Personas - What's The Difference? Relevant Insights. https://www.relevantinsights.com/articles/segmentation-vs-personas-what-is-the-difference/

26 https://chsorens.wordpress.com/wp-content/

uploads/2014/03/product-positioning-practicum1.jpg?w=372

27 https://pt.slideshare.net/arushinayan/nike-perceptual-positioning-map/5

28 https://image.demorgen.be/57430329/width/750/red-bull-kan-voor-hartproblemen-zorgen

29 https://www.shopify.com/blog/what-is-a-distribution-channel

30 Credit: magnetcreative. Stockfoto ID:182864879

31 https://complion.de/media/pages/digital-compliance-blog/salesforce-lizenzierung/168198ab8a-1659103407/salesforce-logo-x1600.jpg

32 https://alstonex.com/wp-content/uploads/2021/10/FMCG-Logos-e1633300841872.png

33 https://www.wearediagram.com/hs-fs/hub/213744/file-2466678536-jpg/blog-files/omnichannel_min.jpg

34 Credit:Eva Blanco. Stock photo ID:1209362043

35 Kuijten, B. (2019). *Nike-app krijgt AR-modus om je schoenmaat op te meten.* iCulture. https://www.iculture.nl/nieuws/nike-fit-augmented-reality-schoen/

36 https://s3-us-west-2.amazonaws.com/courses-images/wp-content/uploads/sites/4052/2019/04/08194200/CommunicationProcessModel3.jpg

37 https://spinsucks.com/communication/pr-pros-must-embrace-the-peso-model/

38 http://simplysianne1.wpenginepowered.com/wp-content/uploads/2020/01/095dfcce-6386-4934-8a3d-682039056e98_PESO-20Model.jpg

39 Copyright: Killian Jouffroy

40 https://www.examples.com/english/marketing-communication-vs-marketing-promotion.html

41 Schrörder, F. (2017). Je videocontent naar een hoger niveau: gebruik het 3H-model. Frankwatching. https://www.frankwatching.com/archive/2017/03/22/je-videocontent-naar-een-hoger-niveau-gebruik-het-3h-model/

42 Credits: georgeclerk. Stockfoto ID:1028191262

43 Credits: Dreamer Company. Stockfoto ID:1281410543

44 https://www.bsl-lausanne.ch/wp-content/uploads/2022/01/content-activity-vs-time.png.webp

45 Pine, Joseph and Gilmore, James (45 2019). The experience economy.

46 https://hbr.org/resources/images/article_assets/hbr/9807/98407_C.gif

47 Credit: Nanci Santos. Stock photo ID:1603700869

48 Credits: IL21. Stockfoto ID:1785531583

49 Credits: Solovyova. Stockfoto ID:1926124983

50 Credit: pxel66. Stock photo ID:486909778

51 Van Eekhout, R. (2020). Customization als middel voor de beste customer experience. robertvaneekhout.nl. https://robertvaneekhout.nl/2020/07/customization-als-middel-voor-de-beste-customer-experience

52 https://cognitivebias.io/uploads/ybias/image-6495a41f59e4d.png

53 https://ds055uzetaobb.cloudfront.net/brioche/uploads/pJVF1pKMtj-supply-and-demand_basic.png?width=1200

54 Credit:Davidagall. Stock photo ID:91165547

55 Credit:piyaphun. Stock photo ID:1222727090

56 The Nielsen Company. (2015). Global Trust

in Advertising Report by Nielsen. Winning strategies for an evolving media landscape. https://www.slideshare.net/slideshow/global-trust-in-advertising-report-by-nielsen/54977064#11

57 Credit:kyonntra - Stock photo ID:1042025046. Credit:Mauricio Graiki - Stock photo ID:1064278966. Credit:piola666 - Stock photo ID:1173154524. Credit: piola666 - Stock photo ID:1139016371

58 https://static.vecteezy.com/system/resources/previews/028/667/072/non_2x/google-logo-icon-symbol-freepng.png

59 https://www.customerscope.nl/wp-content/uploads/2018/07/Buyer-versus-customer-journey.png

60 https://slidemodel.com/aida-model/

61 Court, D., Elzinga, D., Mulder, S. & Vetvik, O.J. (2009). The consumer decision journey. McKinsey Quarterly - McKinsey & Company. https://www.mckinsey.com/capabilities/growth-marketing-and-sales/our-insights/the-consumer-decision-journey

62 Jaffe, J. (2010). *Flip the Funnel: How to Use Existing Customers to Gain New Ones.* John Wiley & Sons Inc.

63 https://theinvestorsbook.com/fcb-grid.html

64 https://phaestus.nl/phaestus.nl/wp-content/uploads/2015/05/fcb-grid.png

65 https://www.signalfox.org/see-think-do-model/

66 https://serpstat.com/files/img/39/uploadfile_1722244303_6366.webp

67 https://www.smartinsights.com/digital-marketing-strategy/race-a-practical-framework-to-improve-yourdigital-marketing/#:~:text=Dave%20Chaffey%2C%20created%20the%20RACE,marketing%20strategy%20and%20implementation%20plan.

68 https://www.smartinsights.com/wp-content/uploads/68 2010/07/RACE-KPIs.jpg

69 CC-BY-4.0. Credit: Hay Kranen. https://commons.wikimedia.org/wiki/File:Vision_Pro_-_Immersed.jpg

70 CC-BY-2.0. 18 June 2024; Attendee Yasmin Bakhtiari uses an Apple Vision Pro headset on day one of Collision 2024 at the Enercare Centre in Toronto, Canada. Photo by Ramsey Cardy/Collision via Sportsfile. https://commons.wikimedia.org/wiki/File:Collision_2024_-_RCZ_9184_-_Apple_Vision_Pro.jpg - Credit: Valen Tino. Stock photo ID:2147535375.

71 Credit:Antikwar. Stock illustration ID:600689988

72 https://www.apple.com/apple-vision-pro/

73 https://d1f5kcwhveewqf.cloudfront.net/uploads/meta-image.jpg

74 Credits:Yongyuan Dai. Stockfoto ID:471592383

75 https://www.apple.com/store

76 Credit:Davidagall. Stock photo ID:91165547

77 CC-BY-4.0. Credit: Hay Kranen. https://commons.wikimedia.org/wiki/File:Vision_Pro_-_Immersed.jpg - Credit:djedzura. Stock photo ID:1310982770

78 https://www.nickelytics.com/wp-content/uploads/2023/04/The-Marketers-Guide-to-Lasting-Brand-Recognition-01-scaled-1.jpg

79 https://trustmary.com/wp-content/uploads/2021/11/Trustmary-NPS-2.png

80 https://media.geeksforgeeks.org/wp-content/uploads/20240202131335/Companies-having-a-good-NPSScore.jpg

81 https://www.wordstream.com/wp-content/uploads/2019/05/b2b-vs-b2c-market-

ing-comparison.jpg

82 https://www.researchgate.net/figure/ The-basic-framework-of-SWOT-analysis_ fig1_261437829

83 https://www.wordstream.com/wp-content/ uploads/2021/07/business-mission-state- ment-vs-vision-vsvalues-vs-goals.png

84 Credit:abalcazar. Stock photo ID:458880621

85 Credit:jetcityimage. Stock photo ID:1386070484

86 https://e7.pngegg.com/pngimag- es/881/46/png-clipart-logo-ikea-graph- ics-brand-font-expression-packagetext-rect- angle-thumbnail.png

87 https://i0.wp.com/ivto.org/wp-content/ uploads/2018/12/macro-meso-micro-fore- sight-cards.jpg?resize=450%2C444&ssl=1

88 https://www.business-to-you.com/por- ters-five-forces/

89 Fenwick, D., Tugrul, D. & Gerdsri, N. (2009). Value Driven Technology Road Mapping (VTRM) process integrating decision making and marketing tools: Case of Internet security technologies. Technological Forecasting and Social Change, 76(8), 1055-1077. DOI:10.1016/j.techfore.2009.04.005

90 https://diffusion-research.org/wp-content/ uploads/2023/05/chasm-theory-curve.jpg

91 https://www.researchgate.net/figure/Por- ters-generic-strategies-Consuunt-2021_ fig1_355351264 .

92 https://i0.wp.com/www.business-to-you.com/ wp-content/uploads/2018/09/Value-Disci- plines-Model.png?resize=463%2C328&ssl=1

93 https://www.researchgate.net/publica- tion/355351122/figure/fig2/AS:1079608413 818882@1634410112764/below-illustrates- the-Boston-Consulting-Group-BCG-matrix-

which-isused-to-analyze-and.ppm

94 https://www.strategypunk.com/content/im- ages/2022/08/StrategyPunk_BCG-Matrix.png

95 https://substackcdn.com/image/fetch/f_au- to,q_auto:good,fl_progressive:steep/ https%3A%2F%2Fbucketeere05b- bc84-baa3-437e-9518-adb32be77984. s3.amazonaws.com%2Fpublic%2Fimages%- 2F3af1fcbf-5ab8-495e-8fa5-909a607793c8_ 879×510. png

96 https://svg.template.creately. com/6bqTrad8z3S

97 https://www.toolshero.com/wp-content/ uploads/2013/10/destep-analysis-model-ex- ample-toolshero.jpg

98 https://substackcdn.com/image/ fetch/w_1456,c_limit,f_webp,q_auto:good,- fl_progressive:steep/https%3A%2F%2F- substack-post-media.s3.amazonaws. com%2Fpublic%2Fimages%2F096e0049-805 4-46d2-a98e-9bf806ed7efa_700×457.webp

99 https://digitalleadership.com/unite-articles/ porters-value-chain/

100 https://strategicmanagementinsight.com/ tools/mckinsey-7s-model-framework/

101 https://www.wallstreetoasis.com/resources/ skills/strategy/mckinsey-7s-model

102 https://prohlik.wordpress.com/wp-content/ uploads/2013/12/plc.jpg?w=367&h=225

103 https://upload.wikimedia.org/wikipedia/ commons/thumb/0/0b/SWOT_en.svg/1200px- SWOT_en.svg.png

104 Credit:Jadiguna. Stock photo ID:1285256292

105 https://www.researchgate.net/figure/ SWOT-Matrix-Framework_fig1_228099104

106 https://gustdebacker.com/downloads/ sfa-matrix/